HIDDEN
HISTORY
of
COLE COUNTY
MISSOURI

Jeremy P. Ämick

THE
History
PRESS

Published by The History Press
Charleston, SC
www.historypress.com

Front cover: The Centennial Mill in later years, when operating as Lohman Milling Corporation. *Virginia Lister.*

First published 2022

Manufactured in the United States

ISBN 9781467152167

Library of Congress Control Number: 2022931671

To the memory of my friends, Gert Strobel and Roger Buchta, who for decades worked tirelessly to document the history of our local area, ensuring the stories of our forebearers were passed down to subsequent generations.

CONTENTS

Acknowledgements

S uch a historical endeavor would not have been possible without the assistance of several gracious individuals. First, I would like to express my gratitude to the late Gert Strobel, whose collection of history from the Lohman area has been of great benefit to me. Additionally, the late Erna Raithel, for her dedicated work in collecting and organizing history pertaining to the Russellville area. My friends Jim and Eve Campbell, for sharing their impressive collection of historical information and photographs. Finally, to all my friends, neighbors and fellow congregation members at St. John's Lutheran Church in Stringtown, for letting me "pick your brains" for many of the stories featured in this book. This is our shared history, of which we can be proud.

INTRODUCTION

Cole County history has occasionally been mistaken to mean Jefferson City history. As the state capital, Jefferson City possesses the appearance of the belle of the ball within local historical circles, having played host to moments in the famed Lewis and Clark Expedition, Civil War activities, persons of interest and a stunning capitol building. But when one travels outside this revered community, one will find numerous small towns and hamlets that have weathered many social and economic storms, all of which possess a rich and bountiful legacy begging to be shared.

In this particular work, the focus was placed on the communities of Russellville, Lohman, Stringtown, Millbrook and Belleville: all towns that are—or were—located in close proximity to one another and have stories that are woven into a unique legacy. Much has been written about towns such as Russellville, which traces its beginnings to the early 1830s, when a wagon train heading to points west broke a wheel. Local lore notes that Enoch Enloe and Lamon Short, pioneers traveling together, were impressed by the natural resources they found in the region that would later become Russellville. Thus, they chose to end their journey, set down roots and build their homes in the area. Many of the families who later joined them helped establish the first churches in the area—Cole Spring Baptist Church and the Russellville United Methodist Church, both of which continue to serve local congregations.

Soon, German immigrants and their families began arriving and established Lutheran congregations, in addition to other places of worship such as a Catholic parish. Not only did these hardy men and women work diligently to carve out farms and build the agricultural capacity of the region, but many also became successful business owners and merchants, constructing roller mills, banks and retail outlets. An economic boost arrived in the early 1880s when the railroad came through Lohman and Russellville—an accomplishment that was accompanied by a tragedy with deadly consequences.

The stories of our forebearers include the forgotten Belleville, one of many towns that have essentially been erased from the landscape. Located a short distance from Russellville, the community's beginnings came in the late nineteenth century, with one man's hope that it might become the site of a railroad depot. When the depot was instead built in Russellville, hopes for the new town quickly dissolved, and all that heralds its existence today is a small Baptist church, a smattering of homes and an inconspicuously small cemetery.

Millbrook was also a community with early hopes boosted by the potential coming of the railroad and becoming home to the once renowned Centennial Mill. Situated a short distance south of Lohman, it was for several years a bustling area of the county with a general store, blacksmith shop and cellars used to store locally brewed beer. When the railroad was planning a spur to be laid through Millbrook, surveyors were driven away from the area by an angry local resident casting rocks. This local woman passionately disapproved of having railroad tracks passing through her property or the community. Instead, the spur was laid through Lohman, which foreshadowed the beginning of the decline of Millbrook.

Stringtown, a community that is situated between Lohman and Millbrook, has little to denote its past outside of the beautiful St. John's Lutheran Church. The town received its name from being "strung out" along a stretch of road for a distance of about four miles. Stringtown was also once home to a Catholic mission, of which only the cemetery remains. It also boasted the residence of the late Dr. Montezuma Hemstreet, who was found brutally murdered after leaving a dance one fateful evening. Like many communities of the era, it once thrived with a saloon, blacksmith shop, general store, post office, stagecoach stop and a log schoolhouse. Charles W. Lohman, a store owner in the early days of Stringtown, later moved his business interests a couple of miles north to an area that became known as the community of Lohman in the early 1880s.

There is much history in rural Cole County, and this book seeks to capture many stories of interest that have ties to the vicinity of Russellville, Belleville, Lohman, Millbrook and Stringtown. It explores fascinating events, people, locations and sundry moments that have been woven into the tapestry of our shared history. Many of these stories, despite having occurred more than a century ago, are still being discussed among local residents. A legacy of simpler times helped create this fascinating composite across a small section of central Missouri. My sincere wish is that you enjoy reading these engaging historical accounts as much as I did the process of researching and writing about them. May all of our rich history—good, bad and otherwise—forever be preserved and passed down to future generations.

Jeremy P. Ämick
Russellville, Missouri
May 2021

CHAPTER I

THE PEOPLE

Dr. William Colbert Hatler

Russellville Physician Convicted of Murder
Received Pardon from Attorney General

Dr. William Colbert Hatler endeared himself to the community of
Russellville through his years of medical practice and was recognized as one
of the city's "oldest and best-known human landmarks" in the book *The
Heritage of Russellville in Cole County* by Reba Koester. However, during the
latter years of Hatler's career, the community was shocked by the news that
their respected physician was arrested for murder by a U.S. marshal.

Born in Henry County, Tennessee, on January 31, 1829, Hatler attended
medical college in Nashville. His obituary indicates he first arrived in
Russellville in 1859 and spent the next few years building his practice. Dr.
Hatler married the former Many N. Mahan on July 4, 1865.

"In the early part of 1870, Dr. Hatler went with his family from [Cole
County] to McDonald County [Missouri]," reported the *Sedalia Weekly
Bazoo* in their February 4, 1890 edition. "He located just on the line of the
Indian Territory, or what is known as Cowskin Prairie, and proceeded to
erect a house."

Dozens of newspaper accounts reveal that Hatler rented a home
from William Sloan, who was identified as half Cherokee, while his own

Dr. William C. Hatler was a physician arrested for a murder and later pardoned by the attorney general. *Jim and Eve Campbell.*

house was under construction. In March 1870, without notice, his landlord instructed him to immediately vacate the home, despite Dr. Hatler's protests that he needed some time to find other accommodations for his family. The *Cedar County Republican* (Stockton, Missouri) reported on February 7, 1890, that Sloan "became abusive to the doctor's family and finally threatened to kill him."

The *St. Louis Post-Dispatch* wrote on February 21, 1892, that Sloan, intent on carrying out his threat to murder the doctor, "went to the house of a neighbor and borrowed a shotgun….[Dr. Hatler] carried with him a small axe to use in case he was forced to defend his life." Further accounts reveal that Sloan was waiting for Dr. Hatler in the house that he was renting. When the doctor entered the home, "Sloan sprang out upon him and attempted to shoot him with the gun."

In the end, Hatler was quicker, raising his axe and striking a deadly blow to Sloan's head. The doctor's actions were viewed as self-defense, and following a brief move to Stoddard County, he relocated his family to Russellville. Dr. Hatler continued his medical practice, believing the horrors of his experiences in McDonald County to be nothing but a bad memory.

Life continued for Dr. Hatler, who was completely unaware he had been indicted for murder by a grand jury in 1885 and that a $200 reward had been issued for his arrest. Two years later, tragedy struck when his wife of twenty-two years passed away, leaving him with a fourteen-year-old daughter (their other daughter passed away several years earlier, when she was only nine years old).

Compassion and demonstration of his medical knowledge helped Dr. Hatler become one of the most revered and trusted physicians in Cole County. His reputation notwithstanding, the news spread like wildfire when, in 1890, a shocked community learned that Dr. Hatler was arrested at his home in Russellville by a U.S. marshal, charged with a murder occurring twenty years earlier.

"Dr. W.C. Hatler, a Missouri physician, now confined in the penitentiary for manslaughter is exciting a great deal of sympathy, and strenuous efforts are being made in Washington, D.C. to induce the president to pardon him," reported the *Medical Review: A Weekly Retrospect of Medicine and Surgery* in their March 5, 1892 edition. "It appeared that in 1870, when he killed William Sloan, everybody looked upon the act as justifiable homicide. It was not until 1891… that action was taken by the authorities…and he was sentenced for three years, and to a fine of $500."

Following Dr. William C. Hatler's death in 1911, Hatler Street in Russellville was named in his memory. *Jeremy Ämick.*

The *Lawrence Chieftain* boisterously reported on May 19, 1892, "[L]ast week [Dr. Hatler] received a pardon from the Attorney General of the United States." The newspaper clarified, "In recommending pardon, Attorney General Miller says: 'The evidence is, to my mind, satisfactory that Sloan was threatening to kill Hatler.'"

Soon, Dr. Hatler was able to restore his life to a semblance of normalcy, and he continued practice of medicine in Russellville. In 1893, he married the former Minerva Ann Schuster; to this union, no children were born. His daughter from his previous marriage, Sadie, married Ben R. Stevens, who became the co-owner of a successful lumberyard in Russellville. The final four years of Dr. Hatler's life were characterized by confinement in his home due to a serious decline in his health. On April 1, 1911, at eighty-two years of age, he entered eternal rest and was buried in the Russellville City Cemetery.

As a physician, Dr. Hatler was committed to the preservation of life, yet unexpected circumstances once forced him to take the life of another in defense of himself and his family—a matter that, for years, haunted him. His contemporaries fought for his release from wrongful imprisonment, and he never lost his passion for being of assistance to his fellow citizens. Hatler Street in Russellville was eventually named in the late doctor's honor. Additionally, his hometown newspaper, the *Russellville Rustler*, printed an impressive homage shortly after his passing.

"[Dr. Hatler] was ever willing to impart his professional knowledge to those in need of his service without the thought of ever receiving any monetary compensation." The newspaper added, "He was broad-minded, liberal hearted, energetic and enterprising…[and] advocated for the betterment of humanity and the community in which he lived."

Dr. Montezuma Hemstreet

"Jack of All Trades" Killed near Stringtown in 1881

The early history of communities such as Stringtown and Lohman is filled with fascinating stories, and some include morsels of intrigue that appear to have been sensationalized during retellings. But others, such as the tragic tale of the late Dr. Montezuma Hemstreet, are imbued with lurid facts that make it difficult to determine whether or not they are colorful works of fiction. Oswald W. Soell was a lifelong resident of the Lohman area and became involved in many civic organizations. He later served as the town's mayor and, prior to his passing in 1972, wrote a brief summary of local history in an effort to ensure it was not lost to future generations.

"About 200 feet on the west bank of the Moreau, a small knoll which was always surrounded on three sides by flood water, when the Moreau was up, here Dr. Hemstreet, a man from Martinsburg, New York, settled and built his home," wrote Soell.

Born in 1819, Dr. Hemstreet was a postmaster in Wisconsin before moving to Cole County shortly after the Civil War. Local oral and written histories both note that although he carried the esteemed title of "doctor," it is uncertain whether he truly had any formal education in the healing arts for treatment of either humans or animals.

"He was a farmer, also acted as a dentist, also legal adviser and lawyer for the people," wrote Soell.

The *Peoples' Tribune* (Jefferson City) reported on July 2, 1873: "Dr. Hemstreet sold 600 pounds of wool…last week. It is well known the doctor raises fine sheep. The wool was of extra quality."

Later newspaper reports indicate that Dr. Hemstreet became deeply involved in local politics and, in 1881, achieved the distinction of being one of the wealthiest farmers in mid-Missouri. Additionally, the economic growth of the area continued to expand after the Missouri Pacific Railroad built a branch through nearby Lohman. It appeared that Dr. Hemstreet, married with two daughters, possessed all of the necessary ingredients for a successful life. Sadly, history reveals that the astute businessman soon fell victim to lustful impulses.

"He was known to have been something of a ladies' man and was reputed to have been involved in relationships with some of the wives of farmers who lived around Stringtown and Lohman," said Don Buchta, a local historian.

On the evening of September 4, 1881, there was a dance in Stringtown at the home of Andrew Bohnenberger. Dr. Hemstreet, in a state of intoxication, passed by on horseback and decided to stop and partake in the party. He soon became involved in a quarrel with some young men in attendance.

"A man named Thompson interfered, and induced [Hemstreet] to remount his horse, going with and assisting him to do so, after which the doctor rode away," reported the *Salem Monitor* on September 15, 1881.

A short time later, Hemstreet was found down the road in an unconscious state, and after being carried to a nearby house and laid on the porch, he died. On September 5, 1881, the day following his death, the *Kansas City Times* reported that his passing was initially perceived as an accident.

"A little before noon today, a report reached here that Dr. Montezuma Hemstreet…had been killed by his horse." The newspaper added, "About a year ago, he had his skull fractured by a refractory mule."

But after a coroner was dispatched to the scene, evidence emerged that his death may have involved foul play. It was determined that someone had struck Hemstreet twice in the head with a hardy oak board, fracturing his skull. This soon led to suspicions he had been killed by a local farmer who had grown tired of the doctor's illicit affair with his spouse.

Missouri governor Thomas Crittenden, on September 24, 1881, issued a proclamation calling for the arrest and prosecution of those responsible for Hemstreet's death and offering a one-hundred-dollar reward. Initially, three suspects were arrested for the murder—brothers William and John

Dr. Montezuma Hemstreet was murdered in 1881 and buried outside the fenced confines of a nearly forgotten Catholic cemetery. *Jeremy Ämick.*

Gemeinhardt in addition to Adam Tierhoff. The Gemeinhardt brothers were eventually exonerated.

The *St. Louis Post-Dispatch* reported on December 18, 1882, that Tierhoff, "who was indicted by a grand jury of [Cole County] for the murder of Dr. Hemstreet…entered a plea of guilty to manslaughter in the third degree." On December 15, 1883, Tierhoff was sentenced to three years in the state penitentiary.

Following Dr. Hemstreet's death in 1881, his body was to be interred in the cemetery adjacent to the former St. Joseph Catholic Church, which sat on a hill overlooking Route C, approximately a quarter mile west of the North Moreau Bridge. Instead, his remains were conspicuously buried outside the fenced cemetery. One story passed down through generations states the Catholic priest serving the parish strongly disapproved of Hemstreet's drinking and womanizing. As such, Hemstreet was not allowed to lie at rest within the holy confines of the cemetery. Another story notes he was placed outside the fence because he was not Catholic.

Local resident Kathryn Linsenbardt explained that shortly after State Route C was moved in the mid-1970s, the county was seeking names for the old highway. In her mind, there was only one name that seemed appropriate.

"Hemstreet was a jack of all trades and had lived in the area," she explained. "The old bridge was always referred to as Hemstreet Bridge by the older residents from Stringtown and Lohman because his house was supposedly just up the hill from it." She added, "When the county sought suggestions to name the old highway, I submitted the name Hemstreet… and perhaps others did, too. Regardless, it now carries the name Hemstreet Road."

John J. Scheperle

Successful Farmer and Mill Owner Leaves Historical Mark in Lohman Area

Born in 1881 in Millbrook, south of Lohman, John Joseph (J.J.) Scheperle was the fifth child and first son of German immigrants John Scheperle and the former Barbara Kirchner. A first-generation U.S. citizen who came of age in rural Cole County, he later made his mark as a businessman and citizen of Lohman. His father was a dedicated member of St. John's Lutheran Church in nearby Stringtown, where young J.J. and his siblings were confirmed and

John Joseph Scheperle (*far right*) married Cynthia Glover at St. John's Lutheran Church in Stringtown in 1903. It was a double wedding ceremony with his older sister, Katherine, and William C. Payne. *David Scheperle.*

attended the church's small schoolhouse. It was at St. John's that, on October 13, 1903, J.J. Scheperle married Cynthia Glover. The nuptials were doubly glorious for his parents since his older sister, Katherine, married William C. Payne during the same ceremony.

According to a booklet printed in celebration of the centennial of St. John's Lutheran Church in 1967, the cornerstone to a new church building was laid on May 14, 1905. This heralded the construction of a brick church that soon replaced the old wood-frame church building. The booklet stated, "All the lumber used in the building of the church was donated in the form of logs, which were milled and prepared free of charge, by the architect and builder, Mr. John Scheperle Sr."

While working alongside his father in the operation of the Centennial Mill in Millbrook and assisting in the construction of the new church building in Stringtown, J.J. Scheperle developed a broad skill set that later helped him become a successful and respected businessman. J.J. Scheperle took over management of the mill, and in 1906, he and his father agreed to move the operation of Centennial Mill to nearby Lohman. This ensured they had the support of the railroad that had been built through Lohman several years earlier. A new mill was soon erected on a plot of land adjacent to the railroad spur. A short time later, the mill equipment was moved from Millbrook, and the old mill was demolished.

In 1908, J.J. Scheperle erected a home for his family north of the mill. The street running along the east side of the home he named Cynthia, honoring his beloved wife. He purchased a significant tract of land east of the mill that he farmed and used to raise livestock. After his wife gave birth to their third child, he hired Sophia Bates to provide assistance around the household.

A Lohman historical booklet printed in August 1976 notes that, although first established in 1882, "it was not until April 7th, 1910 that the town became incorporated." The booklet further explains that at the second meeting of the board of trustees for Lohman, held on May 3, 1910, J.J. Scheperle was elected as a board member. The next few years, a busy period for Lohman, included the construction of a small city jail in August 1910. The bustling railroad community, at the time, had two saloons, a pool hall and a handful of imbibers, whose drunken behaviors frequently warranted an overnight lockup.

A town marshal was hired, and J.J. Scheperle filled the position between 1912 and 1915. In between raising livestock and running the mill in partnership with his friend John Weber, Scheperle also prepared the first

In 1908, Scheperle built this brick house in Lohman for his growing family. Located on Cynthia Street (named for his wife), the house is still used as a residence. *Virginia Lister.*

set of town ordinances and served as the board chairman. When the Lohman Producers Exchange was formed on July 29, 1920, Scheperle again demonstrated that he was inextricably woven into the community at many levels by serving on the organization's five-member board.

"John Eggers…delivered two loads of hogs to J.J. Scheperle, stock dealer at Lohman," reported the *Daily Capital News* on February 24, 1923. The *Jefferson City Post-Tribune* reported on September 27, 1929, "J.J. Scheperle shipped one car of mixed stock to the St. Louis market Thursday."

As a stock dealer, Scheperle had become quite successful and managed to survive comfortably even during the lean years of the Great Depression. However, the coming years were darkened by a moment of shock and loss.

"Miss (Sophia) Bates was found shot to death in the basement of the home of Mrs. J.J. Scheperle for whom she had worked for 25 years," reported the *St. Louis Post-Dispatch* in the February 12, 1934 edition. "Walter Hoffman (who is being) held here for Missouri officers, said yesterday that he had no knowledge of the slaying."

On March 21, 1934, the *St. Louis Post-Dispatch* reported that Hoffman "pleaded guilty yesterday of the murder of Sophia Bates, a domestic, 75, and was sentenced to life imprisonment." He had been captured after stealing Scheperle's vehicle and fleeing to Texas. Hoffman, who had been employed by the Scheperle family, claimed he shot and killed Bates with a .22 rifle after the two got into a dispute over the presidents of the United States. Bates, a native of Russellville, was buried in Pleasant Hill Cemetery in nearby Brazito.

J.J. Scheperle lost his wife, Cynthia, on October 22, 1959. Less than two months later, he also entered into eternal rest. The couple are interred in the cemetery of St. John's Lutheran Church in Stringtown.

"Your story is the greatest legacy that you will leave to your friends," wrote entrepreneur and author Steve Saint. "It's the longest-lasting legacy you will leave to your heirs."

The story of J.J. Scheperle is one of many layers, representing an individual who, while dedicated to friends and family, left behind an impressive history that the years have failed to erode. It is difficult to measure, through an obituary, the mark a person leaves on the world, but Scheperle's legacy thrives through his respected name, the MFA Exchange, Centennial Mill and his family home. Though he has, for decades, lain at rest in Stringtown, many continue to benefit from entrepreneurial and architectural remnants he bequeathed to Lohman.

DR. GEORGE P. TELLMAN

Russellville Dentist Demonstrated Entrepreneurial Spirit and Agricultural Interests

Scores of immigrants coming to the United States in the 1800s were not only trying to escape persecution and economic distress but also seeking safe communities where their children might someday live successful lives. George P. Tellman, the son of German immigrants, fulfilled this parental wish by becoming a respected dentist while also prospering as a farmer and businessman in the Russellville area. Born on a farm near Tuscumbia in 1879, George (G.P.) Tellman was the youngest of thirteen children of Herman Tellman, who came to the United States from Germany when just a young boy. Like many of his siblings, George attended schools in rural Miller County.

"Dr. George P. Tellman, who is on his second year at the St. Louis Dental College, spent the holidays with his father, north of town," reported the *Miller County Autogram-Sentinel* on January 4, 1906. The newspaper added, "George is progressing nicely with his work and will complete the required course next year."

During the summer of 1907, Tellman completed his course of instruction and received his certificate from the State Dental Board. He purchased a dentistry chair from a local dentist and began building his practice in the Tuscumbia area. Within the next couple of years, he moved the headquarters of his burgeoning practice to Russellville but continued to travel to other local communities, such as Tuscumbia and Ulmon, to provide dental services on certain days of the month.

As noted by the *Eldon Advertiser* on November 18, 1909, his practice had grown quickly, and he became one of the first residents of Russellville to purchase an "auto buggy" (automobile). The following year, he was able to acquire several medical appliances that improved his services. These professional developments notwithstanding, it was a personal announcement that astonished local residents.

"Dr. G.P. Tellman and Miss Tillie Cremer surprised their many friends by getting married at the Catholic Parsonage [on May 30, 1910]," wrote Reba Koester in *The Heritage of Russellville in Cole County*. "The only witnesses were Miss Mary Cremer, sister of the bride, and Virgil Leslie of Jefferson City."

The Tellman family welcomed the birth of their only child, a daughter, in the spring of 1911. Though now a family man respected for his dental

Tillie Tellman is pictured at her home, where she and her husband lived in Russellville. Dr. George Tellman, a dentist, owned several farms and was involved in many business endeavors. *Jim and Eve Campbell.*

knowledge and thriving practice, Dr. Tellman still found time to focus on business endeavors, including the purchase of a fruit farm in Arkansas. Soon, the family settled in a brick home built next to Trinity Lutheran Church in Russellville. Dr. Tellman's decision to reside within the city limits did not constrain his interest in agriculture; he acquired several farms around the community, not only raising herds of cattle and hogs but also leasing some of the property for others to cultivate.

In 1920, the doctor again bared his entrepreneurial spirit by joining his brothers and other partners in establishing the Tellman Oil Company, serving as treasurer for the fledgling business.

"Frank Otto of Vienna was here last week interesting parties in the Tellman Oil Co., which has 200,000 acres of oil land leased in Allen County, Kansas," reported the *Miller County Autogram-Sentinel* on December 9, 1920. "The company has bought in another well, making ten in all now producing."

Not every corporate endeavor attempted by Dr. Tellman and his family was successful; the oil company's business license was revoked by the state of Missouri in 1923 and followed by a lawsuit, liquidation of assets and closure.

The Heritage of Russellville in Cole County also revealed the frenetic pace of assorted business transactions that continued to unfold for the restless dentist. "Dr. G.P. Tellman…traded an eighty-acre farm, known as the Fahrni place, to Frank George for stock in the City Drug Store," the book noted.

Despite the intensity of his practice and business dealings, Dr. Tellman often found time for relaxation with friends and family. In 1929, he purchased a new boat for use on the Osage River at the Klug Cave property he owned a few miles south of Tuscumbia. Frequently, the Tellmans invited local friends and businesspeople from the Russellville community to join them, including Mr. C.T. Karr—owner of the Karr Movie Theater—and his wife, as well as Fred Dampf, the town's barber, who married the daughter of the cofounder of the old Russellville Hotel.

When he was fifty-four years old, the active Dr. Tellman, "suffered a broken shoulder blade and other bruises as the result of an attack by a bull at his farm south of town," reported the *Central Missourian* on June 7, 1934. The newspaper noted the doctor "is getting along nicely, although his appearance shows that he had a tough encounter. He was able to come to his office Monday morning and was kept busy most all day telling his friends about the experience."

Twelve years later, in November 1945, Dr. Tellman underwent an operation for cancer in Kansas City. He was living with his daughter and was described as being quite ill and in need of another surgery. On February 22, 1946, the sixty-six-year-old doctor lost his battle to cancer; his wife died nineteen years later, and the couple is buried in Calvary Cemetery in Kansas City.

A young man from Miller County arrived in Russellville decades ago, seeking to build his practice as a newly trained dentist. Dr. Tellman's interests and associations resulted in successful business endeavors, supplemented by spending time with his family and working various farms he owned in the area. The sun has long since set on the life of the doctor and his family, and all that remains of their influence is their home in Russellville and Tellman Road south of town. Through these enduring remnants, local residents are reminded of a fascinating individual with great vision and boundless energy, whose story remains an important part of the intriguing patchwork of the Russellville area.

August Sauer

German Immigrant Turned Russellville Businessman Killed in Accident in 1929

Born in Germany in 1869, August Sauer accompanied one of his four brothers, who made the bold decision to leave their ancestral homeland and immigrate to the United States, the land of opportunity. Once arriving in his newly adopted country, Sauer went on to garner notoriety in the local agricultural industry before meeting with an unexpected and unfortunate end.

"Family lore states that when he came here, he had some 'old family money' from Germany, which he used to buy a 160-acre farm near Millbrook," said his great-grandson, David Sauer.

For August Sauer, 1904 became one of the most memorable years of his young life. First, he purchased the Russellville Roller Mills from businessman Jacob Ritchie. Then he married his fiancée, the former Anna Katherina Hitz, whose family lived in a home across the road from the mill. He operated the mill for a brief time in partnership with Herman Brunning, before purchasing all shares of the business. With an eye to the future, he ensured the mill had the capacity to take on more product than ever before while also purchasing interest in other area flour mills.

August Sauer emigrated from Germany and later purchased the Russellville Roller Mills. He was killed in a vehicle accident in 1929. *David Sauer.*

"His family lived in a large, beautiful home below the mill that had been built for the previous mill owner," said David Sauer. "He and his wife became parents to two sons and three daughters."

A perennial advocate of identifying ways to update milling operations to rise above the competition, Sauer eventually sold his interest in the other mills and focused his attention and efforts solely on his Russellville Roller Mills. "Many of the other mills were getting old and phasing out," David Sauer explained. "He recognized that you either spent the money to update or you closed."

August Sauer soon began marketing his signature brand of quality flour, known as Snow Bank, negotiating deals in St. Louis to have the product shipped throughout the United States. He also supplied flour for institutions within the Missouri prison system. This benefitted the local economy since he purchased and processed wheat grown by farmers in the Russellville area.

Andrew and Mike Doehla of Lohman eventually purchased interest in the Russellville Roller Mills, while Sauer coordinated the provision of another service in the late 1920s, one that would help set him apart from his competitors: deliveries made by truck. According to David Sauer, "He

One of the signature products of the Russellville Roller Mills under Sauer's ownership was Snow Bank flour. *David Sauer.*

contracted with Adam Kirchner in Lohman, who owned a Ford Model AA truck. Weber could pick up the product from the mill and deliver to businesses in the area, rather than them having to come to pick it up themselves."

Also during this timeframe, Sauer began to realize that an evolution in milling was occurring, with electricity coming to Russellville. His foresight led him to believe that the steam engines used to power mills in the area would become outdated and replaced by electricity. One of the ways those in the milling industry shared ideas related to emerging processes and technologies was by attending events such as the Missouri State Fair in Sedalia. On August 20, 1929, Sauer and his wife rode to the fair with one of their sons, Carl.

"August was at the fair on business to promote the mill and bring back information on converting the mill to electric power, while Carl was there to enjoy the fair," said David Sauer. "Toward the end of the day, August and his wife were ready to come home, but Carl was going to stay there for a while. Andrew Kirchner, who made deliveries for August, was getting ready to return to Lohman with a group of people on his truck. August and his wife were able to catch a ride back with him."

Kirchner's vehicle was outfitted with bench seats attached to each side of the truck bed, allowing passengers to lean back against the stock racks. Sometime around six o'clock, the group departed Sedalia, bound for Lohman.

"Three men were killed, a fourth may die, and three others are seriously injured as a result of a collision between two trucks, 2-1/2 miles east of Tipton," reported the *Sedalia Weekly Democrat* on August 23, 1929.

The accident occurred around seven thirty, when the stock racks of a westbound truck carrying a load of peaches struck the stock racks of Kirchner's eastbound truck, ejecting all of the passengers.

"I was told that it was a huge mess, with crates of peaches strewn all over the road along with the passengers of Kirchner's truck," said David Sauer. "Apparently, the mess also included a bunch of August's paperwork, covered in blood."

August was killed immediately in the collision, along with Andrew Weber and Robert Hoffman of Lohman. All three were buried in the cemetery of St.

Paul's Lutheran Church in Lohman. The shares of ownership in Russellville Roller Mills were transferred to Adam and Mike Doehla following Sauer's death. The mill closed in 1933, the result of a drought and the onslaught of the economic distresses of the Great Depression.

"The wife of August Sauer, my great-grandmother, survived the accident," said David. "It was an extremely trying time for the Sauer family, both financially and emotionally. They lost him [and] his investment in the mill, while at the same time the country was falling apart. All the hardships on the farm didn't seem to stop, either. We, as a family, are proud of August's accomplishments, and through the efforts of his children, the family persevered, and many of his descendants remain in the Russellville and Lohman areas."

JOHN JACOB BUCHTA

German Immigrant Became Influential Farmer in Lohman and Russellville

The story of John Jacob (J.J.) Buchta is one of intrigue, featuring a young man who twice immigrated to the United States from Germany and later came into a large sum of money through mysterious means. In later years, he became one of the most recognized citizens of Cole County and played an important role in the establishment of a church that has served Lutherans in the Russellville area for well over a century.

"Jacob, as he was known by our family, first came to the United States with his parents in 1882, when he was only fifteen years old," said his grandson, Don Buchta. "They settled in the Mount Hope area [on State Route U between Russellville and Centertown]."

Don Buchta recalls conversations with his father, who told him that Jacob Buchta returned to Bavaria after being in Missouri for only a couple months. A cloud of mystery surrounds this period; however, family lore notes he soon returned to the Mount Hope area with funds he had acquired.

"We don't know how he came into the money while in Germany," said Don Buchta. "But after coming to Missouri the second time, he left for Los Angeles and used some of that money to purchase an orange grove in an area that has since become Hollywood and Vine."

Buchta later sold the orange grove for a respectable profit and returned to the Mount Hope area, where he had family. Utilizing the profits he made in California, Buchta began purchasing farms and tracts of land

John Buchta, pictured here as a young boy, emigrated to the Lohman area with his family when he was fifteen years old. *Don Buchta.*

Buchta made his home near Lohman and was active in community affairs, helping establish the MFA Exchange and Lutheran church in Russellville. *Don Buchta.*

near Russellville and Lohman. Within a few years, Buchta established himself as a renowned breeder of mules and horses under the business name of Mt. Hope Stock Farm. He also raised other livestock, which he could sell in the larger market of St. Louis by shipping aboard the Missouri Pacific Railroad, which had depots in both Lohman and Russellville.

"The organization of Trinity Evangelical Church, Russellville, Missouri, took place either in September or October of the year 1895," noted the *Golden Jubilee* booklet printed by the church in 1945. "The first deacons elected were John Buchta and Michael Schubert."

Dedicated to his faith, Buchta joined local businessman Michael Schubert on September 12, 1896, in receiving two acres of property purchased from Franz Erhart for establishing a cemetery a short distance south of Russellville. The Trinity Lutheran Cemetery has since served as a final resting site for dozens of members of the congregation. June 12, 1905, was also a special moment in the life of the young farmer: he wedded Lena Christina Schubert of Centertown. The couple raised three daughters and a son, while remaining actively involved in the affairs of the church. They supported the construction of a new brick church that was dedicated in 1912 and continues to serve the congregation of Trinity Lutheran Church.

"I was told that my grandfather was about six feet, two inches tall and weighed over two hundred pounds," said Don Buchta. "He was known to have been extremely strong. There was a time when he and some other people had to do some type of work on the hoof of a horse. Supposedly, my grandfather wrapped his arms around the horse's neck and brought it to the ground so the work could be completed."

The *Jefferson City Post-Tribune* noted on September 14, 1938, that Buchta became "one of the pioneers in the farm organization movement…[serving] on the board of directors of the Cole County Farm Bureau."

J.J. Buchta joined six area farmers in establishing the Cooperative Association No. 13 on May 22, 1920, with its first offices located in the business district of Russellville. According the book printed for the Russellville sesquicentennial celebration in 1988, the association later became known as the MFA Exchange. Though making a decent income through his farm and livestock activities, Buchta found ways to save money while also helping his fellow farmers. On several occasions, he aggregated lime orders for neighboring farmers needing to fertilize their fields.

From 1934 to 1938, Buchta served as an appointed member of the Cole County Highway Commission. The *Jefferson City Post-Tribune* reported on January 3, 1938, that Buchta decided to retire from the voluntary post "because it takes too much of my time."

Time, unfortunately, was not a commodity of which Buchta had a surplus. The seventy-one-year-old farmer died unexpectedly on September 13, 1938, on his farm near Lohman.

"Buchta…had been in bad health for several months suffering from leakage of the heart. He refused to surrender his interest and activities on the farm, however," explained the September 14, 1938 edition of the *Jefferson City Post-Tribune.*

The once unknown German immigrant who later found success as a farmer and livestock dealer in mid-Missouri was laid to rest in Trinity Lutheran Cemetery, which he had helped establish a few decades earlier. His wife, Lena, joined him in eternal rest in 1965.

"When my parents were married in 1934, they lived on one of the farms that my grandfather had purchased," said Don Buchta. "Two years later, my grandfather deeded them the farm and that's the same farm that I live on today." He added, "My grandfather was a strong, imposing figure but was well respected because he was fair in his dealings. Unfortunately, I was an infant when he died and only have the stories of him that I was given by my parents. I just would have liked to have met him."

Alfred Raithel

Lohman WWI Veteran Remembered for Work at Lohman Farmer's Exchange

Several years ago, Gertrude "Gert" Strobel of Lohman began sharing stories, pictures and documents regarding the legacy of her father, the late Alfred Raithel. Possessing many titles during his life, including World War I veteran, manager of the Lohman Producer's Exchange and active member of St. Paul's Lutheran Church, her father left an influence she strived to preserve before it passed into the fog of history.

Alfred Raithel was born on November 23, 1895, and raised on a small farm near St. Martins. His father, Adam, father of eleven children, was a hardscrabble and respected farmer and considered to be one of the pioneer residents of Cole County.

"Although my father was raised in the St. Martins area, he moved to Lohman when he was a young man," Gert Strobel said in a 2013 interview. "His entire life, he attended St. Paul's Lutheran Church and was confirmed in 1909."

For many years, Raithel was employed at the Linhardt & Fischer General Store in Lohman. He was toiling as a farm laborer when he was drafted into military service because of World War I. Strobel shared that, although her father never shared with her many details about his wartime service, records reveal he was twenty-one years old when he was inducted into the U.S. Army on June 20, 1917, and initially assigned to Company M, 356th Infantry. This company was a component of the 89th Infantry Division and completed initial training at Camp Funston, Kansas.

Raithel would go on to serve as a cook overseas from July 31, 1918, through June 14, 1919, and was able to capture several dozen photographs with his camera, chronicling the good, bad and deadly facets of war. Included in the collection were photographs of both American and French flying aces, damaged biplanes and French and German tanks. Raithel also snapped a photograph of the grave of Quentin Roosevelt, an American aviator and the youngest son of President Theodore Roosevelt, who lost his life on July 14, 1918, when his plane was shot down behind German lines.

Rather than allow the snapshots to lie stored away in a musty drawer, shrouded from inquisitive eyes, Strobel donated the photographs to the Museum of Missouri Military History, where they have been catalogued, maintained and enjoyed by others.

While employed as a farm laborer in Lohman, Alfred Raithel was drafted into the army during World War I and served as a cook. *Gertrude Strobel.*

"My father was reassigned to Headquarters Company, 323rd Infantry, with whom he continued to serve as a cook and remained with them until his discharge on June 24, 1919. He then returned to Lohman and began working for the Lohman Producer's Exchange when it was established the following year."

According to a booklet printed in 1976 that highlights segments of Lohman history, "On July 29, 1920, the Lohman Producer's Exchange was formed by a number of interested clubs and local producers. The original five-man board consisted of William Scheperle, president, John J. Scheperle, William Niederwimmer, G.F. Sauerhage and Otto Linsenbardt, secretary."

Albert Heidbreder became the initial manager of the exchange, beginning in 1920, while Raithel was hired to serve as his assistant manager. In 1943, Raithel was promoted to the position of manager.

"Cream, poultry and eggs were bought by the Exchange from the farmers, also wool, which was packed in big wool bags loaned to farmers and later returned," noted Russellville's sesquicentennial book. "The wages were $65 per month for assistant manager and $75 per month for manager," the book noted of the exchange's early history.

"Not long after he returned from the war and began working at the exchange, my father married my mother, Antonia," said Strobel. "I was their only child, born in 1924."

In the early weeks of 1929, Raithel discovered the dangers of working around a grain elevator when he suffered a serious fall; he soon recovered from his injuries. Several years later, the exchange purchased a building that had once housed a restaurant and added a brick structure to the back of it, using the new area as a retail business where they sold items ranging from appliances to cereal. Outside of his work, Raithel and his family remained active members of St. Paul's Lutheran Church. In December 1960, after forty years working for the Lohman Producer's Exchange, he made the decision to retire.

After WWI, Raithel worked at the Lohman Producer's Exchange, eventually becoming manager. He later married Antonia and raised one daughter, Gertrude. *Gertrude Strobel.*

Raithel was sixty-seven years old when he passed away on September 25, 1963, from a heart condition that had plagued him since his retirement. He was laid to rest in the cemetery of St. Paul's Lutheran Church; his beloved wife joined him in eternal rest nearly thirty-one years later. Many decades have passed since the death of the local World War I veteran. His daughter, Gert Strobel, lived until November 25, 2020, passing away at ninety-six years of age. In an interview prior to her passing, Strobel expressed her appreciation for being able to share the history of not only her father's military legacy but his service to the community as well.

"I just want history to be preserved because it was part of the time my dad grew up in that included many fascinating moments," Strobel said. "Dad's story is so interesting, and I am glad that it can now be shared with so many other people who are interested in our past."

Edward Linsenbardt

Lohman Area Farmer Participated in Six Major Campaigns of World War I

Edward Linsenbardt's grandparents departed Germany in the late 1850s and settled near Lohman, where they raised their ten children on a farm in a community of fellow German Lutheran immigrants. Edward's father, Julius, was too young to serve in the Civil War; however, years later, he watched as his son was called upon to fight in a war against a nation from which his family was hardly a generation removed. Born near the community of Lohman on May 16, 1896, Edward "Ed" Linsenbardt was barely nineteen years old, single and working for his father on their farm when the United States made its official declaration of war against Germany on April 6, 1917.

Like many young men his age, Linsenbardt complied with the national mandate to register for the military draft on June 5, 1917. Weeks later, he received official notice of his physical, followed by his induction into the U.S. Army and transfer to Camp Funston, Kansas, for his initial training. In an oral interview conducted in 1978, Linsenbardt said that his parents spoke predominantly in the German language around the home. He noted, "When somebody [came that] you know, an English person, then dad spoke English, he spoke very broken, but at home everything went German."

Linsenbardt possessed a German surname while serving in the military of a nation at war with his grandparents' homeland, and he recalled that some of his fellow recruits occasionally made statements intended as insults, referring to him as "a damned Dutchman." In the early weeks of 1918, Linsenbardt was pulled from his training company and sent to Virginia, along with a group of soldiers needed to fill out the Third Division, which was making preparations to deploy. On April 6, 1918, he departed Newport News, Virginia, aboard the SS *Great Northern*, a passenger ship acquired by the military.

Assigned to Company H, Fourth Infantry Regiment of the Third Division, the newly trained soldiers of the division earned the nickname "Rock of the Marne." As noted in a history compiled by the Society of the Third Infantry Division, a battle occurring near the Marne River on July 15, 1918, helped forge Linsenbardt into a battle-hardened soldier.

Edward Linsenbardt was raised near Stringtown and Lohman. He was drafted in World War I, serving overseas as a messenger with an infantry division. *Roger Kiesling.*

"When flanking units retreated, then Division Commander, Major General Joseph Dickman, told our French Allies 'Nous Resterons La' (we shall remain here)," the society wrote. "This motto is on the 3rd Infantry Division's distinctive insignia."

Although the division was described as being successful in the battle, Linsenbardt explained the dangers of soldiering during this timeframe. "I went through six battles over there, I got six Bronze Stars and I didn't think I would ever see home anymore," he said. "I was a messenger. I didn't kill anybody but I had to deliver the messages. I done a lot of crawling and running and some of the shells, they landed…well twice it happened—a shell landed close by me and it didn't go off. Bullets…I could feel the wind of them, you know, the machine gun bullets that give you the chills."

According to Linsenbardt, the closest to hell on earth he experienced in the war came during the division's participation in the Meuse-Argonne Offensive. This offensive evolved into the deadliest campaign of the war for the American Expeditionary Force.

"According to records, the division sustained more than 16,000 battle casualties when the counting was completed on November 11th [1918]," noted Donald Grabert in his book *History of the Third Infantry Division*, published in 1988. Linsenbardt said that, shockingly, only 14 soldiers out of his company of 250 survived the battle.

Prior to the armistice, Linsenbardt was frequently selected by his lieutenant to accompany him on patrols. At first, the Lohman soldier silently questioned why another messenger was not chosen but he soon came to suspect the officer's underlying motive.

"He wanted to know about my schooling and whether I could speak German and all of that," Linsenbardt said. "[S]ome others (messengers), they were stronger and better qualified if they had got into a fight, [but] later I got to thinking—I have an idea he figured in case we would get captured by the Germans, I could help him because I could speak a little German."

Following the armistice, the division became part of the occupational forces and eventually established post-war headquarters in Andernach, Germany. Military records indicate that Linsenbardt departed Brest, France, aboard the USS *Henderson* on August 13, 1919, arriving in Brooklyn, New York, twelve days later. Receiving his discharge on September 2, 1919, Linsenbardt married Viola Schubert of Lohman two years later. The couple raised two daughters and spent the next several years farming land near the area where they had been raised.

Viola passed away in 1969 and was laid to rest in the cemetery of St. Paul's Lutheran Church in Lohman. Linsenbardt was ninety-two years old when he died in 1988 and was laid to rest next to his wife. Linsenbardt explained why he, like many veterans of the First World War, chose to remain silent about their service in the years after returning home. "I didn't say much about my experiences over there as some of the people…they didn't believe it," he said. "And I told one of them the last battle we [were] in, there was only fourteen left. He said, 'I don't believe that.'" Years later, when an acquaintance from Lohman asked Linsenbardt why he did not share stories from his time in the service, he responded, "I thought, 'What's the use?' A lot of folks will think I'm just lying [although] some boys will [brag] about it."

CORNELIA LINHARDT

Nineteen-Year-Old Lohman Woman Wins National Cherry Pie Baking Contest in 1936

During the Great Depression, the baking skills of a nineteen-year-old woman from Lohman earned her a national honor that included a trip to Washington, D.C., visits with Missouri senators and an unforgettable presentation from the First Lady of the United States. Her brief moment in the spotlight was not only accompanied by nationwide newspaper coverage but also came with offers of marriage from strangers.

Born in Lohman on December 4, 1916, Cornelia Linhardt grew up with five brothers and was the daughter of A.N. "Nick" and Anna (Schoch) Linhardt, owners of a general store in town. She received her early education at the Lohman School, but since it only went through the eighth grade, she drove daily to Jefferson City High School to finish classes.

"Miss Linhardt, a junior, was selected Friday as winner of the local contest for students in food classes taught by Miss Lou R. Dillon, home economics instructor at the high school," reported the *Sunday News and Tribune* on February 9, 1936. "At Chicago, Miss Linhardt will compete with other high school students from virtually every state for cash prizes."

The nineteen-year-old Linhardt and her chaperone/food instructor at Jefferson City High School, Mrs. Lou Dillon, departed Jefferson City aboard the train on February 20, 1936. Linhardt had been baking pies since she was fifteen years old, and the young woman from Lohman was elated to be traveling to Chicago for a contest sponsored by the National Cherry Week Committee.

In the March 1936 edition of the *Hotel Morrison Digest*, Linhardt wrote that the trip was her first experience leaving the boundaries of Missouri. The excitement surrounding the contest reached a crescendo almost immediately upon her arrival with the making of new friendships. She soon "became

Cornelia (Linhardt) Fischer was a high school junior when she won a national cherry pie baking contest in 1936. She received a one-hundred-dollar prize and a silver trophy at the White House from Mrs. Eleanor Roosevelt. *Natalie Fischer Young.*

acquainted with the nine other girls [selected as finalists] and their chaperones from the nine other states. Each girl was interested in the other and we eagerly and anxiously awaited the days in which we were to be together." Linhardt continued, "Friday morning marked the day of the contest. Each girl, after a hearty breakfast, stepped into the elevator and glided up to the Bungalow floor where we made our pies."

A short time later, after eating a luncheon, the group of ladies returned to view their pies, which had been baked by "an experienced chef." They were then led into a large room filled with judges, reporters and photographers, where each lady stood behind the pie she had prepared and waited for the judge's declaration of victory. "A few seconds of silence and then Mrs. Gray said slowly but surely, 'The winner of the contest is—'Miss Missouri,'" Linhardt wrote. "Oh, I could have dropped."

She was presented with a one-hundred-dollar check and then taken shopping so a new dress could be purchased for her to wear for upcoming celebratory activities. The next couple of days were a whirlwind: Linhardt was feted at a banquet, participated in a question-and-answer session on a radio program and departed Chicago for Washington, D.C., to visit the U.S. Capitol buildings, Mount Vernon and Arlington. The highlight of the trip came when she was escorted to the White House to meet with Eleanor Roosevelt. During the brief visit, the First Lady presented young Linhardt with a large silver trophy.

"For many years, the trophy was displayed in a case at Jefferson City High School," said Natalie Young, Linhardt's daughter. "It has since been returned to the family and I now have it."

Referencing a photograph of Linhardt displaying her winning cherry pie, the *Ruston Daily Leader* printed a statement seemingly predictive in nature: "After men see this picture, Miss Cornelia Linhardt of Lohman…may be deluged with marriage proposals, for not every young lady can both smile so nicely and bake a prize pie."

Natalie Young said of her mother's experiences after returning to Lohman, "Because she won the national contest, her picture was printed in

Cornelia Linhardt wedded Arno Fischer in Lohman in August 1941. *Natalie Fischer Young.*

newspapers nationwide. She began receiving letters from men throughout the U.S. containing marriage proposals," she chuckled.

Linhardt returned to Lohman with an unanticipated level of notoriety but went on to finish high school and began working for an insurance company in Jefferson City. Despite the many offers of marriage she received, Linhardt fell in love with and married Arno Fischer—a farmer from Lohman—in August 1941. The couple raised a son and a daughter. Linhardt became a homemaker in addition to possessing a talent for music, occasionally playing organ at St. Paul's Lutheran Church in Lohman and providing piano lessons to many local youths over the years. In 1970, the fifty-three-year-old passed away from cancer; she is buried in the cemetery of St. Paul's Lutheran Church in Lohman.

Natalie Young realizes all that remains of her mother's brief moment of fame are newspaper clippings tucked in a scrapbook and a time-tarnished silver trophy. However, her mother's fascinating experience, she maintains, is a story worthy of being preserved and shared.

"I mentioned it to my oldest daughter, and she didn't know anything about it," Young said. "It's a story that I want to reacquaint my family with because it has kind of been forgotten over the last few decades." She concluded, "Back then, you often didn't travel very far from home, but I find it amazing that this nineteen-year-old girl from Lohman could be picked out of a group and thrust into the national spotlight because of a pie-baking contest."

Howard Wyss

Russellville Area WWII Veteran Served as Bombardier Aboard B-24 Liberator in China

Howard Ewing Wyss was raised the youngest of five children on a small farm near Russellville in Moniteau County, Missouri. Following his graduation from high school in nearby California in 1935, he spent the next few years working a number of jobs as the country strived to recover from the Great Depression. Howard met his future wife, Berniece Parrish, while the north and south Moniteau County youth gathered at a freshwater spring on Sunday afternoons, said his son, Mike Wyss. Howard asked her to a show in California, and they soon began dating.

The couple married on December 22, 1940, while Wyss was employed driving a truck for his older brother's transportation company. At the time, much of their work came from delivering supplies used to build the hundreds of buildings on the developing Fort Leonard Wood. There was little time to celebrate their new marriage because, only two months earlier, the twenty-five-year-old Wyss was mandated to register for the military draft. On February 17, 1941, the *Jefferson City Post-Tribune* reported that he was among twenty-three local inductees scheduled to report to "Jefferson Barracks to undergo examinations in preparation for one year's army training."

From there, Wyss was assigned to the Thirty-Fifth Division and transferred to Camp Robinson in North Little Rock, Arkansas, for a year of training. Several months later, he decided to pursue a military direction other than the infantry when he volunteered to serve in the U.S. Army Air Forces.

"I think he decided if he was going to war, he'd rather be above it all," said Mike Wyss.

The veteran's daughter, Nancy Kruse, added, "He was going to become a pilot but failed the test because of his depth perception. That's when he went on to train as a bombardier on the B-24s."

The aviation cadet attended Army Air Forces Bombardier School near Big

Howard Wyss is pictured with his wife, Berniece, in the early 1940s. Drafted in WWII, Wyss served as a bombardier aboard a B-24 Liberator in China. *Nancy Wyss.*

Spring, Texas. Throughout the next several months, he completed a number of ground courses and target missions over a practice area while learning to use technology such as the Norden bombsight, a highly classified instrument that increased bombing target accuracy.

Sadly, on July 28, 1943, Wyss's older brother Nobel, who was a radio operator aboard a B-17 Flying Fortress, was killed when his aircraft crashed twenty-eight miles south of Fort Morgan, Colorado, while on a training mission. Both Wyss and his wife traveled to mid-Missouri for the funeral.

Becoming part of the ten-man crew of a B-24 Liberator—a four-engine heavy bomber—Wyss was transferred to the West Coast to participate in patrol missions from locations such as Blythe Army Airfield. Their duties included searching for enemy submarines along the coast between Santa Monica and Santa Barbara. His wife, Berniece, moved to California to be with her husband.

"Sometime later, he left the States with a group of twenty planes and two hundred men heading for duty in China," said Mike Wyss. "On the way over, his plane developed engine troubles and had to land in Cairo, Egypt, for a few days for repairs." He continued, "While there, they were able to visit the pyramids."

Nancy Kruse remarked, "When they finally made it to China, our father volunteered for as many missions as possible because once you reached a certain number of missions or flight hours, you were sent back to the States. He wanted to get back home to mom as quickly as possible."

On a small piece of paper, Wyss wrote that he was stationed near a small town along the southeastern coast of China, from where he and his fellow crewmembers of the 374th Bombardment Group flew missions in search of Japanese ships. He penned, "We sank seven ships, at least one loaded with Japanese troops."

Wyss explained that, because they did not have the protection of American troops, they were soon driven further inland by Japanese forces. They continued flying coastal missions, although from a much greater distance.

According to Nancy Kruse, "He was often in the belly turret of the plane and some of these missions might last ten hours or longer."

Howard Wyss's older brother, Nobel, was killed during a stateside training mission in 1943 while serving as a radio operator on a B-17 Flying Fortress. *Nancy Jobe.*

Later in the war, Wyss's crew was among a group of aircraft sent to bomb Japanese ships in the fortified Takao Harbor in Taiwan. Because of the heavy defenses encountered, they circled from a safe distance while the aircraft in their group were individually dispatched on bombing runs.

"They believed it was too dangerous to send all the planes at once," said Mike Wyss. "My father was in the ninth of ten planes and, along with the tenth plane, watched as the first eight were shot out of the sky." Somberly pausing, he added, "Fortunately, he and the final plane survived their bombing run."

When Wyss returned to the States in late 1945, only two of the twenty planes and one hundred of the two hundred crewmembers with whom they had traveled overseas remained. Following his discharge, he and his wife moved briefly to Rolla, where the veteran attended college on the GI Bill. In later years, the couple raised a son and daughter while building a successful meat processing and locker plant in the Russellville community, in addition to pursuing other professional endeavors. He remained in the Air Force Reserve, retiring as a major in 1960.

Wyss and his wife have since passed, but his children remarked that it was not until his final years that he chose to share snippets of his military service. For most of his life, he focused his attention on being a father and investing countless hours in earning a decent living to support his family.

His daughter, Nancy Kruse, commented that the family always thought of their dad and grandfather as a very hardworking and dedicated gentleman; working six days a week from early morning until late evening was the norm. "His faith, courage, wisdom and work ethic will always be our inspiration," she said.

Mike Wyss added, "We have a great-grandfather who served in the Civil War and know nothing about his service. For us," he paused, "it's about making sure these stories are not forgotten; it's not just our family's story, but also that of so many other families in our great country who have loved ones who served."

Chapter 2

Education

The Birth of Russellville Schools

School System Finds Earliest Beginnings in a Small Log Cabin

Russellville was first surveyed in 1838, establishing a community that began to grow exponentially in the coming decades. As the years passed, one-room schoolhouses popped up throughout the rural countryside, serving as the primary means of education for local youth prior to the consolidation that resulted in the larger school districts seen today. Remembrances of the first school in the Russellville area were printed in the 1976 book *The Heritage of Russellville in Cole County*. Within its pages, George T. Connell, born in 1861, was quoted describing the only school that existed during his childhood.

The school was located approximately one mile south of Russellville, and Connell noted that his late grandfather, Basil McDavitt, who is considered one of the pioneers of the community, served as the teacher of his small class.

Connell said, "I started to school my first year with a few children in a house made of logs, daubed with mud and with hewed puncheon floors. The seats were made of split trees as there were no tools in those days for making finished wood products."

The late L.A.B. Leslie, former postmaster and area historian, chronicled that the first school in Russellville was established in 1882 and consisted of a one-room frame structure. However, classes were later moved to the old Methodist Church building once located on Jefferson Street.

One of the earliest schools in Russellville was held in the former Methodist Church building. A two-story brick building was erected in 1899, providing more space for classes. *Jeremy P. Ämick.*

For a brief time in the early 1900s, Professor William Rhoads conducted grade school classes at the church building for students in the immediate vicinity of Russellville, while children in the outlying areas attended one of the many one-room schoolhouses. Rhoads later made the decision to leave his career as an educator, becoming a farmer on three hundred acres outside of town.

"By 1899 the local paper, dated February 24, states, 'Nearly every voter in this district realizes the fact that we must have a new school building, and to this aim we are still striving,'" noted Russellville's sesquicentennial book. The newspaper was also quoted as stating, "We do not want a little two by four school house but a good roomy building for the benefit of non-resident pupils as well as the resident pupils."

A large, two-story brick structure with four classrooms was erected on a piece of property located on North Smith Street. Writings by L.A.B. Leslic note that in 1910, one year of high school credit was offered for the first time, with eleven students availing themselves of the new opportunity. There was a suspension of high school offerings until the fall of 1914, when newly created consolidation laws, which suggested the closure of several local one-room school districts, became the basis of disagreements between community members.

Leslie explained, "The consolidation and activation of a high school nearly tore the community apart. Merchants were boycotted, neighbors would not speak to each other and elections were held every thirty or sixty days to vote for or against levies."

"All the schools in the Russellville consolidated district opened this September 1915, for the first time since consolidating of the several districts at this place," wrote Reba Koester in *The Heritage of Russellville in Cole County.* "In addition to the regular grades, a two-year high school course was taught."

Koester noted that not only were there improvements to the library and laboratory during this period but the school also boasted an impressive enrollment of 231 students, including 26 participating in the new two-year high school course.

William Rhoads was an early teacher in the Russellville school system, leading grade school classes in the old Methodist Church building. *Martha Jobe.*

The school welcomed several teachers throughout the next few years. In 1916, Archie Russell was hired as a teacher after the previous instructor, James B. Musick, was compelled to resign following an altercation with the school board. Russell was born in the community of Decatur, once located five miles south of Russellville. He had previously taught at Cottage Grove School, a one-room building located south of Russellville that was destroyed in a tornado in April 1916. The year following his arrival at Russellville, the twenty-seven-year-old Russell was drafted into the U.S. Army and deployed to France in World War I.

For a brief period following his discharge, Russell was employed as a mail carrier in the Russellville area but in 1920 resigned this position to return as a teacher for the school. In 1922, Ms. Amy Griffin was hired to teach classes, giving the school the resources to now offer a third year of high school.

Under the leadership of Superintendent Roger V. Smith, school enrollment rapidly increased "and the primary grades were moved to a rented building where a Catholic School had been conducted," according to the Russellville sesquicentennial book. The late Freeman Kraus, prior to his passing, shared details regarding his early educational experiences at the rented school building.

"I started to school in 1920, when I was six years old," Krause wrote. "My first year was at a small school that the school board had rented from the Catholic Church. They were not having church school at that time. It was not a very big building." He added, "Russellville had a real nice grade school building....They used the two rooms [upstairs] for high school and the lower rooms for upper grades. I went two years to the small rented building."

In the coming years, the district's earliest beginnings in a small log cabin south of town would nearly be forgotten. In light of rapid expansion, the school district would need funds to purchase the property and materials to build adequate facilities, where they could continue to provide a decent education to area students.

Russellville School District Grows into Two Campuses

When a six-year-old Freeman Kraus started grade school in Consolidated District No. 1 in Russellville in 1926, older students attended classes in a relatively modern two-story brick building. However, because of overcrowding from a growing student population, his first educational experiences were in a small building that was rented from the Catholic church. In the years before his death, Kraus reflected on his early education, writing that his first teacher was Bertha Hitch, who originated from the Brazito area and taught with the Russellville school district for many years.

"At Christmas [1926] our teacher promoted Nelda Schubert and I to the second grade, which didn't set too good with the rest of the class," Kraus reminisced. "The boys said she flunked all but us that year, but that was not right."

A few years before Kraus and his handful of classmates embarked upon their grade school education, grander plans were implemented to ensure there would be adequate facilities to support the ever-growing student population, while also expanding the educational offerings in the district. Roger V. Smith, the superintendent at Russellville in the early 1920s, was elected the Cole County superintendent of schools in 1923. On May 1, 1923, despite Smith's best efforts, a proposed tax levy to support the construction of a larger school, and to expand the high school from three to four years, failed to pass.

"Citizens of the Russellville Consolidated School District desiring a four-year high school course there are not deterred by the election Tuesday," reported the *Daily Capital News* on May 3, 1923.

According to Russellville's sesquicentennial book, "Under the leadership of Mr. Smith, (members of the school district) undertook the task of building by [public] subscription. During May and June (1923), $7,000 was raised by the citizens; thus, with the state aid they were assured a fund of $9,000."

The expansion of the district was supported by the donation of a five-acre tract of land on the south side of Russellville. Within only a few months, a new high school building had been completed.

"Amid impressive ceremonies yesterday morning, the new Russellville High School building was formally dedicated," wrote the *Jefferson City Post-Tribune* on January 2, 1924. "The newly dedicated edifice is an $18,000/two-story and basement brick structure. It was built by subscription and donated labor. There is not a penny of debt in it." In sincere appreciation for the efforts of County Superintendent Roger V. Smith, he was presented with a gold watch and chain by the citizens of Russellville.

The next few years brought a medley of progress for all grade levels. The large, two-story structure on the north side of town was often full of students from the primary grades, while high school students received instruction in the newer facility on the south side of Russellville.

L.A.B. Leslie wrote that between 1929 and 1931, high school was discontinued, but through the efforts of E.S. Bond, who was both a school board member and secretary of the district, high school was soon reestablished.

"Russellville…is to have a new $96,000 school building," reported the *Iberia Sentinel* on December 14, 1939. "Work started last week on the structure. It is a WPA (Works Progress Administration) project."

The old high school building was demolished on the property on the south side of Russellville to accommodate the new, larger school building that would host both the elementary and high school. The following year, 1940, the two-story brick building in the north of town was also demolished, with many of the materials salvaged for other construction projects. All grades moved into the new facility in 1942. Since that time, there have been several additions and improvements made to the property; many of these enhancements were necessitated by the consolidation of one-room school districts.

Enrollment continued to increase, and in 2000, a new high school was built outside the city limits, west of town, on more than thirty acres donated by L.A.B. Leslie. The elementary and middle school remains on the south side of the city, on property belonging to the school district since 1924.

Above: Constructed in 1899, this brick school served Russellville-area students until 1940. It was demolished, and many components were salvaged for use in a newer school building on the south side of town. *Jim and Eve Campbell.*

Right: The blue bell under the marquee sign at Russellville High School once hung in the bell tower of the community school, demolished in 1940. *Jeremy Amick.*

There is little evidence of the transition the school district made from a small log cabin south of town to two sprawling campuses. However, an item was donated to the high school that helps link the current educational institution to its extensive history.

"My dad's aunt and uncle, Herbert and Ruth Hahn, acquired the bell from the brick schoolhouse that was torn down [in 1940]," said Jeff Payne. "During their estate sale in the late 1990s, it was purchased by Ben and Dorothy Goodin in Brazito and used as a yard decoration. The Goodins decided the bell needed to return home to Russellville and donated it to the school in 2012."

The bell, manufactured by C.S. Bell Company of Hillsboro, Ohio, has been painted blue and is mounted under the marquee and message board by the entrance of Russellville High School along State Highway C. Though only a simple metal object, the bell rang boldly for many years, but now silently denotes that the past and future of the school district remain connected. The bell is an object through which to share with future students the history and growth of their local education system. In the words of former President Theodore Roosevelt, "The more you know about the past, the better prepared you are for the future."

JAMES B. MUSICK

Former Russellville Teacher Became Leader at St. Louis City Art Museum

In 1899, when small one-room schoolhouses dotted the rural landscape, the citizens of Russellville constructed a two-story brick building, where local children attended grade school. For many years, all classes were instructed by a single teacher, including one whose career was propelled to lofty heights because of friction with the school board over a disciplinary issue.

"Students were offered one year of high school credit for the first time in the fall of 1910," wrote the late Erna Raithel in Russellville's sesquicentennial book. "No high school subjects were offered again until the fall of 1914."

James Boggs Musick was born in Lupus, Missouri, on August 12, 1891. He later lived in the Lohman area and went on to earn his degree in education from the University of Missouri. He was hired by the school board to serve as the professor at the school in Russellville in 1913, but troubles emerged the following year.

James Musick was a teacher at Russellville when asked to resign after a disagreement with the school board. He later became secretary of the City Art Museum in St. Louis. *Jim and Eve Campbell.*

"Some of you will recall when the school board at Russellville asked for the resignation of Prof. [James] B. Musick, which was given and accepted by Cole County Superintendent J.S. Lumpkins," explained Ruby Koester in the chapter highlighting the year 1914 in her self-published book *The Heritage of Russellville in Cole County*. "The trouble at the school arose over the whipping of Revis Enloe, the fourteen-year-old son of [Edward Eugene] Enloe. He was given a rather severe punishment and the father complained to the school board. The differences between Mr. Enloe and Prof. Musick were settled and school duties resumed."

Despite Musick's maintaining order and discipline in the classroom as part of his duties and having gone to the effort of working matters out with Enloe's father, the school board demanded that Musick punish some of the other students who had committed similar offenses. Musick refused to comply with the board's wishes, resulting in their demand that he resign from his position. The educator conceded, and another teacher was hired to finish out the remaining three months of the 1913–14 school year.

By no means did the loss of his employment negatively impact Musick's career in the long term. Following his resignation in the early weeks of 1914, he moved to St. Louis and was hired as a doorman by the City Art Museum. Within a few years, he demonstrated his competencies and was hired as the museum's secretary in 1922.

"As an experiment to determine whether people wish to visit the City Art Museum in the evenings, it has been decided to open the doors this evening… for all who wish to visit the exhibits," reported the *St. Louis Globe-Democrat* on October 12, 1928, denoting Musick's community engagement efforts.

His brief experiences as an educator in Russellville influenced Musick's views; he frequently stressed that visitors were often hesitant to ask questions about the museum's displays. It was his belief that when a person was educated on the background of a particular exhibit, it enhanced their level of appreciation and enjoyment.

On February 26, 1932, less than three years after the advent of the Great Depression, Musick felt obligated to defend the museum's expenses and special tax dispensation in a letter to the editor printed in the *St. Louis Star and Times*. In a period when government expenses were publicly scrutinized, Musick maintained, "It is always necessary at any given date to have a sufficient balance to pay the Museum's operating expenses until the next tax collection."

His duties as secretary again found him arguing in 1938 on behalf of a measure to continue the property tax that funded the museum. Although the country was only beginning to lift itself from the economic mire of the Great Depression, Musick asserted the museum's budget would be cut in half if the proposed measure were to pass. As he explained to a reporter with the *St. Louis Star and Times*, half of the revenue received from taxes went to operating expenses and administrative costs, while the remaining balance was used to purchase art objects.

For years, Musick gleaned personal satisfaction from his hobby of collecting rare stamps and ancient maps. Additionally, he explored an interest in writing by penning an article for the book *George Caleb Bingham* in 1935 and, later, by serving as director of the Missouri State Historical Society.

A highlight in his life came when he published the book *St. Louis As a Fortified Town* in 1941. Through this work, Musick revealed his detailed knowledge of the history of St. Louis while sharing many unique maps of the area, earning him the title of "an illuminating cartographer" from the *St. Louis Globe-Democrat* on October 18, 1941. His work at the City Art Museum would be interspersed with historical research and writings during the next four years while his health, sadly, fell into rapid decline.

"James B. Musick, secretary of the City Art Museum, was found dead in his bed late this morning at his home," reported the *St. Louis Post-Dispatch* on May 29, 1945. "Cause of death has not been determined, but members of the family said he had suffered from a heart ailment for many years. He was fifty-three years old."

Musick's remains were transported to Columbia, where one of his sisters resided. He was laid to rest in the city's Memorial Park Cemetery.

The late political leader Nelson Mandela said, "Everyone can rise above their circumstances and achieve success if they are dedicated to and passionate about what they do." In that spirit, Musick, from the shattered hopes of a career in education, ascended from the ashes of adversity, using it as the stepping-stone to a career that he enjoyed and pursued with great passion, intuition and focus.

LOHMAN SCHOOLS

Lohman Community Possesses a Rich Legacy of Public and Parochial Schools

In the mid-1880s—approximate to the time Charles W. Lohman moved his stock of mercantile goods from Stringtown to a village forming a couple miles north along the new branch of the St. Louis-Jefferson City-Kansas City Railroad—the area's first non-parochial schoolhouse was erected. The community, which became known as Lohman, strived to provide a good education for local youth until consolidation changed matters several decades later. The first Lohman School was a concrete building erected on the northwest side of town. Historical accounts note the building was utilized for more than thirty years, at which time it was determined a newer schoolhouse was needed.

"From 1882–1904, Pastor Finkenscher conducted full-fledged parochial school with teachings in secular as well as religious subjects," noted the booklet printed in 1952 for the one hundredth anniversary of St. Paul's Lutheran Church in Lohman.

The first Lohman School was erected in the 1880s and used for classes until 1917. The walls of the school still stand on private property on West Lohman Road, concealed by trees and growth. *Virginia Lister.*

During this twenty-two-year period, children of St. Paul's were not sent to Lohman School but instead attended the parish school. In 1904, with end of full-day school being held at the church, children of St. Paul's started receiving their education at Lohman School. In the years that followed, many of the students from St. Paul's would have to suspend their studies at Lohman School to attend a full-time religious school at the church for the two years prior to confirmation. This was often followed by their return to Lohman School to finish out their eighth grade education.

There remained many connections between the Lohman School and St. Paul's Lutheran Church in the coming years. On May 23, 1917, construction began on a new school building in Lohman, highlighted by the efforts of Gus Linsenbardt—a member of St. Paul's—who served as foreman in the construction project.

The new brick "building included two rooms, two cloak rooms, and an entrance hall," according to Russellville's sesquicentennial book. "At one time, the large room was divided and was used as a high school."

There was also a basement dug for the school and, for the first three or four years, the floor remained a dirt base. When concrete was laid for the basement floor, the work was accomplished through the use of a hand concrete mixer. Gus Linsenbardt later became the contractor for the construction of the new St. Paul's Lutheran Church (the current church building), which was dedicated on November 6, 1924. Linsenbardt's building skills were again embraced by the school board a few years later.

"The Lohman Public School will be wired for electric lights sometime in the near future," reported the *Jefferson City Post-Tribune* on August 14, 1930. "Gustav Linsenbardt has the contract for furnishing the material and doing the work."

Clarence Reichel, who served three years as superintendent at Lohman Public School, announced his candidacy for Cole County superintendent of schools in early 1931. When the election was held two months later, he lost to Roger V. Smith by 1,500 votes. Smith had once been superintendent for Russellville schools.

The class sizes in Lohman grew to such an extent that, in the fall of 1931, a total of three teachers were employed. Growth in student population may have signaled robust educational offerings in the community, but the following year would result in depressing moments due to illness.

"The sudden appearance of scarlet fever in the Lohman school, which alarmed this community temporarily the past three weeks, has been checked," reported the *Daily Capital News* on February 21, 1932.

Built in 1917 by Gus Linsenbardt, the second Lohman School building now serves as the Lohman Community Center. *Jeremy Ämick.*

In an effort to halt the spread, four students were confined to their homes, resulting in no reported complications or further illnesses. Months later, however, a new illness would have much more serious consequences for the small community and again result in the closure of the school for a brief period.

"2 NEW CASES OF DIPTHERIA ARE REPORTED," bawled the headline of an article appearing in the *Jefferson City Post-Tribune* on October 3, 1932.

The newspaper noted that while health authorities raced to immunize children, two new cases of serious infection were identified in Lohman. The article revealed that Clarence Meier, an eight-year-old boy who attended the Lohman School, was stricken with the illness and died on October 1, 1932, while being transported to the hospital in Jefferson City.

Lohman School continued to be used to deliver an educational experience to youth for the next several years. During World War II, the building became the location where men of draft age completed their registrations under the mandate of the Selective Training and Service Act of 1940.

"From 1944 to 1946, I attended Stringtown School—a concrete building that is now gone," recalled Lohman native Gus Fischer. "When that school closed, I attended third grade at Lohman School from 1946 to 1947."

The fascinating story of Lohman School—which had served the community for nearly seven decades—came to an end in the mid-1950s, at which time state consolidation laws resulted in its closure, and the students were transferred to nearby Russellville. In later years, members of the Lohman community united for the preservation of the historic brick school building. It is now used as a community center where many local events are hosted, including community barbecues and Fourth of July celebrations.

When one now enters the former Lohman School, its walls no longer echo with the scrapes of chalk across a blackboard, the admonishment of a teacher telling students to cease idle chatter or hushed giggles resulting from a pigtail being dipped into an inkwell on a desk. Yet the building has now become a symbolic slate upon which the community has written memories of their educational background, providing an outlet for many local residents to celebrate and share the rich legacy of forgotten rural schools.

ENTERPRISE SCHOOL

One-Room Schoolhouse Served Millbrook Area Students for Several Decades

"The [one-room] schoolhouses were in most communities the first public building to be erected, and became an arena for social, political and religious meetings," wrote Leidulf Mydland in an article appearing in the *European Journal of American Studies* in spring 2011. "Altogether more than 200,000 one-room schoolhouses were built in the rural areas of the USA, mostly in the Midwest, where more than 90,000 of these quite simple buildings were erected."

Counted among this impressive list of unadorned educational institutions is the former Enterprise School. Once located along a now-condemned country road in a rural area of Cole County, the school for several decades served students who lived in the vicinity of Millbrook. Shortly after the Civil War, Mathias Hirschvogel, an Austrian immigrant who became a farmer in the Millbrook area, donated an acre of his property for the intended purpose of building a schoolhouse. The donation was made with the agreement that should the school ever close, the property would revert back to the farm.

"The school was built and named Enterprise," according to Lenora Doehla and Dorothy Scheperle's reflections, printed in the 1988 book

Located between Russellville and Millbrook along a condemned county road, the former Enterprise School stands in a wooded area on property owned by the Kautsch family. *Jeremy Ämick.*

celebrating Russellville's sesquicentennial. "Andrew Weber [later] purchased the farm with the same understanding."

Historical records reveal that members of the school board later discussed building a new school at a different location, but when Weber disclosed that he was not interested in purchasing back the property, the plans were abandoned and the original Enterprise School remained.

"In 1922, there were thirty-eight students with Theodore Engelbrecht as teacher," stated Russellville's sesquicentennial book. "School board members were I.C. Simmons, president; William A. Amos, clerk; N.A. Doehla and George Scheperle."

The school served students from the Millbrook community for several decades, and due to certain factors, such as its distance from homes scattered across the rural landscape, the enrollment oscillated from as few as five to as many as seventy students. In 1932, the school had a meager enrollment of twelve pupils.

"Many had to walk three to four miles to school," explained Russellville's sesquicentennial book. "This fact contributed to poor attendance, causing a few to reach the age of twenty-one before graduating." Teachers "boarded with neighboring families" and, just like the students, "walked to and from school."

Susan Scheperle Schenwerk's grandfather, George Scheperle, was a member of the school board, while her father, Elwyn Scheperle, attended the school during the Great Depression. In her father's effects, she found a photo of the school from 1908 that featured the teacher, Ms. Mary Berry of Russellville, and her thirty-one pupils. Berry later married Andrew

Ms. Mary Berry, a teacher at Enterprise School, is pictured with her class from the 1907–08 school session. *Susan Scheperle Schenewerk.*

Blochberger and was only fifty-eight years old when she passed away in 1944. She was laid to rest in Enloe Cemetery outside Russellville.

For several terms in the late 1920s, Ms. Dorothy Payne served as the school's sole teacher. As a child, she had herself gone through the eighth grade at the small Cottage Grove School before graduating from nearby Russellville High School in 1925. Payne continued her education at Central Business College in Sedalia and the State Teachers College in Warrensburg before marrying Charles Hahn. In later years, she taught at schools in Cole, Moniteau and Miller Counties for a total of thirty-two terms. Dorothy Payne Hahn was 101 years old when she passed away in 2007 and is buried in Eldon City Cemetery.

"The Enterprise School [session] closed last Wednesday," wrote the *Jefferson City Post-Tribune* in the April 23, 1929 edition. "Miss Lennora Doehla received her diploma, passing the eighth grade."

Doehla, who was ninety-one years old when she passed away in 2004, is responsible for preserving a significant amount of the early history of Enterprise School.

"The Enterprise School opened Tuesday," reported the *Jefferson City Post-Tribune* on September 5, 1929. "The building has been entirely remodeled during the summer vacation."

Initially, the small schoolhouse had a brick exterior, but as evidenced in a handful of photographs, the bricks were at some point covered with stucco. The county road that ran in front of the school was condemned in 1940, and by the spring of 1945, enrollment declined to the point that Enterprise School was closed permanently.

Andrew Weber, who owned the property surrounding the one acre upon which the school building sits, was among three individuals killed in a vehicle collision east of Tipton in August 1929. His brother-in-law, William Kautsch, later purchased the property so that his sister and nephews (Weber's widow and children) could remain living there.

"I was told that in the early 1950s, after the school had closed, my grandfather purchased the one acre of school property at an auction," said William Kautsch, grandson and namesake of the farmer who purchased the property from Weber. "Over the years, the building had been used for storage, and you can still see where the cistern and flagpole were located."

All too often, the locations where one-room schoolhouses stood are now empty, without even the friendly whisper of a building to remind the world of the important role they served in a bygone educational tradition. However, though revealing a few wrinkles from years of weathering, along with busted-out windows and cracked stucco, Enterprise School continues its quiet residence in the shaded forest in rural Cole County, refusing to relinquish its rich legacy of instructing students.

Marjorie Morrow

Second Grade Teacher Fondly Remembered by Friends, Colleagues and Former Students

Centuries ago, Greek philosopher Aristotle made the intuitive observation of those who teach: "Educating the minds without educating the hearts is no education at all." His statement could easily have applied to the late Marjorie Morrow, who, after spending decades teaching second grade in the Russellville area, is still warmly remembered by former students and coworkers even years after her passing.

Born in 1930 and raised in the small community of Enon, Morrow attended a nearby one-room school before finishing her education at Russellville. Sadly, her fifty-two-year-old mother passed away during the latter half of her junior year of school in 1946. The May 30, 1947 edition of the *Daily Capital News* reported, "There was an overflow crowd for the graduation exercise held in the school auditorium," where Morrow was the valedictorian among her seventeen classmates at Russellville.

Choosing to pursue her interest in education, she began attending Central Missouri State College in Warrensburg. In 1950, she continued to demonstrate her scholastic aptitude when inducted into the Alpha Phi Delta sorority, honoring female students who had exceptional personal qualities and earned good grades. While attending summer sessions in college, she also received early educational experience and a modest income through teaching at the former one-room Enon School. This busy time of her life was complicated after her brother, more than a decade older, perished in an unexpected tragedy.

Marjorie Morrow taught for forty-three years, mostly at Russellville Elementary School. The second grade teacher is fondly remembered by former coworkers and students. *Cole R-1 Schools.*

"Vernon Morrow was killed when his car collided with a trailer truck on Highway 66, near the Villa Ridge cutoff, early Sunday morning," reported the *Washington Missourian* on May 11, 1950. "His remains were taken from the undertakers in Union to his home in Russellville for burial."

"I grew up in California, Missouri, so I only knew Marjorie for the last twenty-eight years of her life," said Tina Dearixon-Weber, a close friend. "After the tragedy of losing her brother, I believe that is part of the reason she may have never married and had children, because she felt that she needed to be with her father."

Consolidation of smaller school districts resulted in the closure of Enon and other local one-room schools, but Morrow was hired to teach the fourth grade class at Russellville. She was soon assigned to the second grade class and continued to teach at that level for the next few decades.

"When I was in early elementary school, she was my teacher and rode our school bus to school for a while," said Wanda Larimore. "She lived on her mom and dad's farm outside of Enon and was always very calm in nature."

Morrow's attendance in summer courses resulted in her earning a bachelor's degree in elementary education in 1956. Through all the busyness of her own studies and teaching, Morrow remained a dedicated member of the Enon Baptist Church, using her refined talents as a pianist to support the music ministry of the congregation.

Maribeth Russell, who taught at Russellville schools for many years, remembered that Morrow not only attended parties and get-togethers with fellow teachers outside of school but also willingly lent her talents for special events. "When I got married, I asked her to play piano at our wedding ceremony and she did a lovely job. She was always the life of the party and could bring a smile to your face." Russell added, "She was an excellent teacher; I know that for a fact. I would often overhear high school students talking about who their favorite teacher was and, time and time again, their response was Ms. Morrow in the second grade."

A student in the second grade class during the 1973–74 school year, Gina Linsenbardt Prosch, recalled fond memories of Morrow reading excerpts of the book *Heidi* to the class after lunch and the youthful comments made by classmates regarding their teacher's name.

"Her middle name was Marie and I remember that a bunch of us girls thought it was neat that all of her names started with *M*," said Linsenbardt Prosch. "We joked that she probably didn't want to get married since she might have to change her name to something that started with another letter."

Jana Thompson began teaching first grade classes at Russellville in 1974. Excited about the new opportunity, she quickly came to respect Morrow while also discovering that her coworker did not restrain herself from sharing any thoughts on her mind.

"As a new teacher, we received our indoctrination and were told to dress professionally," said Thompson. "I remember walking down the hall with Mrs. Morrow—and I called her that for the longest time—while wearing nice clothes with a skirt. She turned to me and said, 'That skirt is way too short for you.'" Mirthfully, Thompson added, "I never wore that skirt again."

Thompson noted that a previous first grade teacher had not adequately prepared her students to enter the second grade level, much to Morrow's dismay. Realizing she was facing a high bar of assessment for academic achievement, Thompson was pleased by the comments she received at the end of her first school year.

"Marjorie wanted me to do well and send her kids that were ready," said Thompson. "At the end of my first year, she told me I had done a good job, which meant a lot to me."

Morrow retired from Russellville in 1991 and, like many in retirement, suffered some health problems during the last few years of her life. On March 6, 2014, the eighty-three-year-old former educator passed away and was laid to rest in Enloe Cemetery near Russellville.

With a fondness cultivated from years of friendship, Maribeth Russell remarked, "She definitely had high expectations of her kids in the classroom because, when you have such expectations, she knew that the kids would rise to meet them. Her classroom environment was also well controlled, but the students loved her, and she was very much respected by her peers."

GROVER SNEAD

Spent Decades in Education and Administration in Mid-Missouri

As a young child growing up in a small Missouri town, Grover Snead was imbued with a formidable work ethic while working on his parents' farm. During his youth, he also acquired an appreciation for education when attending a one-room school in the area. In later years, he applied many of these experiences in his thirty-four-year career as an educator and administrator for schools in Jamestown and Russellville.

"My father was born near Denver, Missouri, in 1917 and was raised there until his older brother graduated from the eighth grade," said Virginia Brizendine, the older of Snead's two daughters. "Then the family moved to New Hampton, Missouri, where he graduated from high school."

In the summer of 1935, after finishing high school, Snead enrolled at the University of Missouri–Columbia. Four years later, he earned a bachelor's degree in agriculture and went to work for the Salem Hybrid Seed Corn Company and, later, a poultry hatchery in Jefferson City. His early experiences also included giving farm reports on KLIK radio.

"Our father met our mother, Mildred 'Millie' Herndon, on a blind date while he was in college, and they married in 1940, shortly after he graduated," Brizendine recalled. "Soon, World War II began, and our father went for a physical but was disqualified because of a heart murmur."

Theresa Maxwell, Snead's youngest daughter, added, "He worked for the Carnation Milk Company for three years in Arkansas, Tennessee and Maryland as a field representative and receiving station manager. He finally decided to leave the company and became the county extension agent for Ralls County."

With the war coming to an end, Snead acted on his interest in teaching in 1946, providing farm training in Moniteau County to returning service members under the G.I. Bill. His training consisted of classroom instruction for enrolled students on Saturdays, supplemented by visits to their individual farms during the week. His daughters noted that their father first entered in a farm partnership with his father-in-law, then purchased his own farm in the Jamestown area in 1947. In the mid-1950s, realizing that farming required an investment he could not afford at the time, Snead chose to become a teacher.

"Dad went to [University of Missouri] in 1957 and earned his teaching certificate," said Maxwell. "He was hired as the agriculture teacher at Russellville in 1958."

In addition to his educational endeavors, Snead's life was marked by an unyielding pace of activities. This included community involvement as a Mason, service as president of the Russellville Lions Club, membership at Russellville Baptist Church and appointment as a director with the Peoples Bank of Moniteau County in Jamestown.

According to Maxwell, while her father taught at Russellville, vocational agriculture programs around the state began to shut down and migrate into industrial arts programs. Her father, seeking to ensure his future in the school system, returned to college and earned his master's degree in education from MU in the summer of 1963.

Grover Snead began his career in education as a vocational agriculture teacher at Russellville High School. He later became superintendent at both the Jamestown and Russellville schools, retiring in 1982 after thirty-four years of dedicated service. *Virginia Brizendine.*

"He was always preparing for that next step," said Maxwell. "Also, he was interested in the administrative aspect of teaching because he always liked organizational work, planning, solving problems and the financial side of things."

In 1964, Snead was hired by the Jamestown school board to serve as the school's superintendent. He held that position until 1968, at which time he became superintendent at Russellville, although he was initially reluctant to accept the job.

"I quickly found out the high school students were largely out of control," Snead wrote in later years. "One of the worst incidents had been a meatball fight in the cafeteria. I was also told that the high school principal wouldn't leave his office during the lunch period."

The high school principal soon decided to move on, and the new superintendent contacted Jack Brumley, who had taught at Russellville a year prior to Snead moving to Jamestown.

"I recognized his qualities and liked him," Snead wrote about Brumley. "I called Jack and told him I had news for him….I told him he would be moving to Russellville." He added, "This turned out to be my most important decision. For fourteen years we worked together without one cross word."

The Snead family moved to a home in Russellville but maintained the farm in Jamestown, which they rented out to farmers in the area. His wife, Millie, not only worked as a homemaker but also used her time in Russellville to substitute teach and finish her home economics degree at Lincoln University.

Snead turned sixty-five years old in 1982 and chose to retire from education after more than thirty-four years in the profession. He and his wife eventually moved to the nearby community of California, where he helped prepare farm taxes for others in his spare time and traveled with friends and family. The former educator was ninety-one years old when he died, and he was laid at rest in the Masonic Cemetery in California on Good Friday in 2008.

Brizendine explained that, even though the school board granted her father permission to "swing the paddle" when discipline was needed, he took time to address the concerns of others, earning him an enduring respect from students and the community alike.

"Dad would talk to anyone at the drop of the hat," Brizendine said. "He might be locking up the school after a game or a meeting, and somebody would come up and ask to speak with him. It might be an hour later, and we would be sitting in that cold car ready to go home, but he was patiently listening to what they had to say." She added, "He liked people…and when you spoke to him, you got his full attention."

HAROLD PRIEST

Longtime Russellville Coach Also Served as Principal and Superintendent

While pursuing an education at Arkansas State College in Jonesboro in the mid-1950s, Harold Priest worked his way through school at a local print shop. Like many young people in college, he was initially uncertain of his educational focus, but he soon set his sights on becoming an educator—a career choice that would later provide fond memories for students at several Missouri high schools.

"Harold graduated from college with his bachelor of science degree in education," said the late educator's wife, Sally. "He had gone to college with the son of the superintendent of the high school at Climax Springs (Missouri) and was offered a job there [in 1955]."

Priest taught social studies and history in addition to coaching baseball and softball. Shortly after embarking upon his teaching career in the small

Camden County village, he met Sally Moulder, and the two were married in December 1956.

Sally recalled, "After two years at Climax Springs, Harold was one of three teachers requesting a raise of $30 per month. After the board of education denied their request, the teachers left the school, and he was hired to teach at Cole Camp [in August 1957]."

The budding educator taught classes while also serving as a basketball coach. Throughout the next year, he gained local notoriety for leading the small Cole Camp basketball team to a 29–2 record for the season. Clyde Penick, who was the superintendent that initially hired Priest at Climax Springs, had been hired as superintendent at Russellville. At the end of the 1959 school year, Penick hired Priest to come teach and coach for the rural Cole County school. Sally recalled, "For the first year, he was the coach and taught physical education for Russellville High School."

Prior to the start of the school year, in May 1959, the Priests became parents of a daughter, Connie Sue. The following year, Priest made the transition into administration when hired as high school principal. He continued, however, to coach in addition to his new responsibilities in administration. The school's proximity to nearby Jefferson City lent itself to an opportunity for Priest to continue making an investment in his own education. In the summer of 1962, Priest was awarded a master of education degree at Lincoln University.

Decades earlier, in 1937, a four-year-old Priest had his right eye surgically removed because of a tumor. For the rest of his life, he wore a glass eye—a device resulting in a perceived stern "look" that inspired many humorous memories among several former students.

"I was a seventh grader and had such a terrible headache, so I went to his office for an aspirin," recalled former Russellville student Jerry Koestner. "He was reading a book and looked up at me [with his glass eye] and asked, 'Koestner, what do you need?'" Chuckling, Koestner went on, "He was still reading with his other eye, and it scared me so badly that I forgot what I came there for. He simply said, 'Well, Jerry, if you remember, come back.'"

Sharon (Jones) Young recalls Priest serving as the sponsor for the Russellville High School class of 1961. On one occasion, the class was lined up in the hallway, and she decided to sit down on one of the pedestal ashtrays in the front lobby. (At the time, adult visitors were allowed to smoke in the building.)

"Mr. Priest came down the hall and I quickly stood and knocked the round metal ring off the ashtray," Young remembered. "It went rolling down the hallway and I ran after it with my heart pounding because I knew I was in trouble…but he didn't say a word and just stood there with that look."

Priest and his wife were filled with unfathomable sorrow at the passing of their five-year-old daughter and only child, Connie Sue, in December 1964.

"The community of Russellville, with the cooperation of the Eugene and Versailles High Schools, will hold a Memorial Benefit Basketball game…in honor of Connie Priest," reported the *Sunday News and Tribune* on January 10, 1965. Proceeds from the game and a community supper would be "turned over to Priest, who is the basketball coach at Russellville High School and has built the Indians into a Central Missouri power."

Priest remained at Russellville until 1966, at which time he became superintendent of schools at Lowry City, Missouri. While there, he

Born in 1933, Harold Priest attended college in Arkansas before entering a career in education. He spent many of his formative years as a coach and principal at Russellville High School. *Cole R-1 Schools.*

enrolled in college in Warrensburg, earning his educational specialist degree. In 1968, he became superintendent in Belle, remaining there for the next decade.

"Harold was superintendent for a couple of years at Sherwood School District in Cass County before going to Linn as their superintendent," said Sally. "After five years at Linn, he decided to retire since he had thirty years in education."

Shortly after Harold's retirement, the Priests moved to Jefferson City, where Harold sold real estate for a brief period and enjoyed the occasional game of golf. The eighty-five-year-old retired educator passed away in 2018; he was laid to rest near his daughter in Enloe Cemetery near Russellville.

Sally Priest remembered that in later years, she joined her husband for many class reunions and alumni events at Russellville High School, fondly observing as students reminisced and shared memories of the educator who had provided a positive influence in their young lives.

"All of those years he served at Russellville really brought him close to the students," she said. "Not just because of his work as the principal and coach, but he basically fulfilled the role of school counselor until one was hired." She added, "He knew all of the kids, and when he moved on and became superintendent at other schools, he no longer had that close connection with the student body."

Erna Raithel

Positively Influenced Her Community as a Dedicated Christian and Educator

Mid-Missouri is blessed by women whose dedication to education and volunteer work has created a legacy that continues to resonate throughout the community. On this distinguished list is the late Erna Raithel, whose contributions to molding young minds in local schools and within her beloved church serve as the basis for pleasant reflections among those who remember her selfless, giving spirit.

Born in 1919 and raised on a farm between Russellville and Lohman, Erna Raithel and her eight siblings became first-generation U.S. citizens; their father had emigrated from Bavaria in the 1890s. Like many coming of age in rural communities in the early twentieth century, she was instilled with a deep and abiding work ethic.

"She went to nearby Russellville elementary and high school," said Raithel's niece, Becky Verslues. "The family attended Trinity Lutheran Church in Russellville, and she remained with that congregation her entire life, volunteering for many roles within the church." A fourteen-year-old Raithel was confirmed as a member of Trinity Lutheran Church in 1934.

A fourteen-year-old Erna Raithel is pictured in her confirmation photograph from Trinity Lutheran Church in 1934. *Trinity Lutheran Church.*

Inspired by her first grade teacher, Hazel Schubert, Raithel resolved to pursue a career in teaching. After graduating from Russellville High School, Raithel enrolled at the Central Missouri State Teachers College in Warrensburg (now University of Central Missouri) to help usher this aspiration into reality.

"She actually raised and sold turkeys to help pay for her college," said Verslues. "In 1940, she began teaching at Lohman School and, in the summer months, attended college. She often rode to classes with Margie Fahrni and Thelma Kraus [other well-known area educators]."

Raithel taught at Lohman until 1945, the same year she graduated with her bachelor's degree in education from Warrensburg. She was then hired as a teacher at Simonsen Junior High School in Jefferson City, remaining there for the next two years. In 1947, a twenty-eight-year-old Raithel returned to her alma mater, Russellville High School, teaching English, general math, literature and American history. The school's yearbook from 1954 notes she was eventually appointed school principal. Raithel again demonstrated her commitment to continuing education by earning her master's degree in English from the University of Missouri in 1954.

"My Aunt Erna began teaching at the Jefferson City Junior College in 1954 and was there for two years," Verslues said.

According to the August 8, 1957 edition of the *Sedalia Democrat*, the junior college closed after the 1957–58 academic year, partially attributed to the integration of the student population at nearby Lincoln University. Following the closure of the junior college, Raithel taught drama, English and an adult education program at Jefferson City High School, eventually becoming chair of the English department.

 The next several decades were highlighted by a medley of teaching and volunteer work but also included her decision to purchase a home in Russellville, where she lived for many years with her sister, Augusta.

According to Verslues, "She became friends with Gert Raithel of Lohman, who she always said was a distant relative. Gert attended the Lutheran church in Lohman and didn't marry until later in life, while Erna attended the Lutheran Church in Russellville and never married, so they shared a common background and interests."

In 1963, Raithel penned some highlights about an adventure she and her friend Gert experienced during a trip to Europe. It was a busy itinerary that included stops at locations in France, Belgium, the Netherlands, Denmark, Germany, Austria, Switzerland, Liechtenstein, England and Scotland. During the trip, she visited the Robert Raithel family, cousins who lived in Munchberg and Stambanch, Germany. After returning from the joyful trip, Raithel wrote, "A trip to Europe, especially England, was a dream fostered for many years; and this past summer that dream finally became a reality." She added, "It proved all that I hoped for. There were many memorable days and impressions, some impossible to describe."

Raithel's involvement at church mirrored much of her daily educational endeavors—selfless service as Sunday school superintendent, membership in the parish education committee and development of a curriculum guide and teacher training program for Sunday school instructors.

Her multiple passions were soon succeeded by assorted accolades.

A first-generation U.S. citizen born in 1919, Erna Raithel pursued a career in education and was active with Trinity Lutheran Church in Russellville. She helped preserve the histories of both Russellville and her beloved congregation. *Becky Verslues.*

"Miss Erna Raithel has been selected as one of five 'Women of Achievement for 1969' by the Jefferson City Chapter, American Association of University Women," reported the *Sedalia Democrat* on January 14, 1970.

The Jefferson City Community Teachers Association recognized her with the "Outstanding Teacher Award" for 1981–82.

Retiring from Jefferson City High School in 1985 after achieving thirty-five years in the educational profession, Raithel found peace and enjoyment in tending the flower garden at her home. She also helped preserve local history by editing and writing much of the Russellville sesquicentennial book, in addition to anniversary books for Trinity Lutheran Church. In the final years of her life, she held fast to her Christian faith and remained active in her church despite developing infirmities. On April 2, 2008, the eighty-eight-year-old retired educator passed away and was laid to rest in Trinity Lutheran Cemetery near Russellville.

Becky Verslues grew very close to her aunt in later years, learning to appreciate the kind and gentle nature she graciously shared with the world on a daily basis.

"My mother was killed in a car accident when I was only thirty years old, and Erna became a second mother to me," Verslues said. "We often did things together, and I got to see firsthand the kind heart she possessed." Smiling, she concluded, "Throughout her life, she carried out her Christian faith and was very generous to all people. There truly is no way to accurately measure the wonderful influence she had on the lives of others."

Chapter 3

Building Business

Centennial Mill

Historic Lohman Mill Possesses Impressive Legacy Dating Back to 1856

Historical documents reveal that John W. Kirchner first opened a mill along the South Moreau in 1856, near what is now the junction of State Highway D and Millbrook Road, a few miles south of Lohman. Several years later, John Scheperle, who immigrated to the United States from Germany with his parents in 1847, settled near the mill in a community he later named "Millbrook."

"On February 18, 1870, [John Scheperle]…was married to Anna (Barbara) Kirchner at Zion Lutheran Church, Cole County, Missouri, by the Rev. Carl Thurow," wrote Palmer Scheperle in the book *History of the Scheperle (Schepperle) Family in America.*

The book goes on to explain that John Scheperle acquired experience as a millwright while previously living in Ohio. As a young man, he is believed to have worked at a mill owned by his brother-in-law, located near Millbrook, Ohio, which became his inspiration in naming the Cole County community where he later settled.

Shortly after his marriage, a business-minded Scheperle purchased a half interest in the mill of John Kirchner, his new father-in-law. The next several years were marked by hard work and expansion of the steam-powered grist mill. However, tragedy struck one evening when the building mysteriously caught fire and burned to the ground.

Centennial Mill in Lohman has a legacy dating back to the first mill built by John Kirchner in Millbrook in 1856. Pictured is the Centennial Mill erected in Millbrook in 1876. *Virginia Lister.*

"It was thought to be arson but was never proven," noted Palmer Scheperle. "The loss was estimated at $7,000."

Construction on a new $12,000 mill began in 1876, and although the company was often referred to as the Kirchner and Scheperle Mill or the Millbrook Roller Mills, it was soon given a more permanent name. The rebuilt business was called "Centennial Mill" since construction began during the year of the country's centennial celebration. The *State Journal* reported on December 20, 1878, that Scheplere and his father-in-law had completed the new mill, erected using brick and stone, and were only waiting on the metal for the roof. The newspaper stated, "It will be provided with all the latest improved machinery and be one of the finest mills in the country."

Clarence Payne, a grandson of John Scheperle, wrote in the *Sunday News and Tribune* on July 18, 1971, that Millbrook became a thriving community with "a rather large trade area including a post office, blacksmith shop, general store, and handle factory."

According to Payne, the town of Millbrook essentially grew up around Scheperle's flour mill, which was later supplemented by a "lumber mill and wool carding where raw wool was brought to be processed."

John Scheperle and his oldest son, John Joseph (J.J.), operated the mill for the next several years while J.J.'s sisters assisted with duties in the woolen mill. In the late 1870s, when it appeared as though a boom might arrive with a planned railroad spur through Millbrook, unexpected circumstances resulted in an important business decision. Family oral histories passed down through the years claim that John Scheperle's mother-in-law, Margaret (Rockelman) Kirchner, was not enthused over the potential disturbances presented by a railroad running through the Millbrook community.

The undaunted woman is reputed to have collected buckets of rocks, throwing them at the railroad surveyors when they came near her property. Apparently, the railroad then decided to move their line a few miles south, through the community that became Lohman. Lacking convenient access to the freight-hauling capabilities of the railroad, the Scheperle family realized the days were numbered for their Millbrook business.

"Although Lohman had a flour mill as early as 1887, it was in 1906 that the Centennial Mill of Millbrook was moved to Lohman by John Scheperle and his son, John J. Scheperle," in the words of a booklet printed in 1976 highlighting Lohman's early history.

Rather than dismantle the mill and move it brick by brick, a new building was erected parallel to the railroad tracks in Lohman. The steam engine and other equipment used in milling operations were moved from Millbrook, and the old mill was later demolished.

"Original stockholders in this mill were the Scheperles, John Weber, Andy Doehla, Martin Doehla, and Mike Weber," noted the Lohman history booklet. "The…Lohman Milling Corporation grew out of this earlier organization being incorporated January 26, 1932," producing a reported two hundred to three hundred barrels of flour per day.

J.J. Scheperle, who married the former Cynthia Glover in 1903, moved to Lohman to oversee the business and built a house on a small hillside north of the mill, likely using bricks from the old mill in its construction. There was once a pond on the west end of the Centennial Mill to supply water for the steam engine used in milling. The pond was eventually drained and filled; the steam engine was scrapped during World War II. Storage buildings have been erected on the site of the former pond, and the steam engine was replaced by a diesel engine.

"After the mill was incorporated in 1932, some of the owners were Oswald Soell, Emil Kepelmann and Eddie Soell," said Gus Fischer Jr. "Eddie Soell was killed in an automobile accident, and I ended up buying out his part of the mill."

Fischer noted that at the time he bought into the mill, his brother, Raymond, was already a half owner. For the next several years, the brothers, in their business partnership, operated Lohman Milling Corporation as

The equipment and contents of Centennial Mill were moved to Lohman in 1906 and the old mill later demolished. Pictured is the mill in later years, operating as Lohman Milling Corporation. *Virginia Lister.*

primarily a wholesale feed operation. Some of the products they offered included cattle feed, hog feed, salt blocks, protein blocks and fourteen types of dog food.

"We later built Centertown Feed and Farm Supply along the railroad tracks in Centertown, where we had access to shipments from the railroad and also sold such agricultural supplies as fertilizer," said Fischer. "We then added bulk supplies like groceries, sugar, cocoa, cereal and some canned goods."

The Centennial Mill has been used for many purposes since moving to Lohman and was purchased in 1984 by Ray and Virginia Lister to store HVAC equipment for their business. Since that time, the mill has transitioned from the role of agricultural business to more of a museum, providing insight into the early days of mill operations. The building has long been in retirement but holds the distinction of being the only surviving mill in Cole County. Virginia Lister hopes the building is able to survive well into the future as a tool to educate and connect others to their ancestors and an important agricultural legacy.

"I love the history of the site and hope it can be placed on the National Register [of Historic Places] someday," Lister said. "Not many of these mills have survived, but I hope the Centennial Mill can be maintained and its rich story of people and surrounding communities shared with generations to come."

MICHAEL SCHUBERT

Orphan Rose from Dire Beginnings to Become Respected Russelville Businessman

Stretching along Railroad Avenue in downtown Russellville is a large storefront, crowned with a section of red bricks that boldly displays the name Schubert. This structure, which is well over a century old, serves as a memorial of sorts to an enterprising young man who contributed greatly to the development of a church and the early growth of the surrounding community.

Michael Schubert was born near Taos in 1859. He experienced hardship in his early years when his father, John, died during the early part of the Civil War. The young private, a member of the Cole County Home Guards, had been on guard duty by a railroad bridge in Osage City when he was struck by a train on August 7, 1861. Several years later, his mother died from smallpox, leaving young Michael and his sister, Kate, orphaned. Throughout the next several years, he buckled down and worked hard to earn an education.

In her book *The Heritage of Russellville in Cole County*, Reba Koester wrote that the formal education Schubert received "amounted to only a few years in the public school and a few months in a private German school."

"At the age of 24, he was associated in the mercantile business at Decatur," stated Russellville's sesquicentennial book. Decatur was once a thriving community with a mill, hotel and other businesses, located south of Russellville along the South Moreau Creek.

Frederick "Fritz" Steffens, a German immigrant and businessman in Decatur, took the young Schubert under his wing and taught him how to operate a successful business. Schubert also garnered from Fritz an interest in the funeral profession. After spending four years in Decatur, he moved to Barnett and purchased a stock of goods so that he could operate his own store. Schubert fell in love and, in 1889, married Mary Schneider from his hometown of Taos. Sadly, Mary was only twenty-seven years old when she died in 1893 and was laid to rest in Big Rock Cemetery in Barnett. Still reeling from the loss of his beloved, Schubert chose to build his business in the nearby community of Russellville, which was experiencing a period of unprecedented growth because of the railroad.

The next several years were a whirlwind of activity for the entrepreneur. In 1895, he became one of the organizers of the Russellville Exchange Bank, the first financial institution of the community. For two years, he worked as a cashier at the bank, but then chose to focus on other possibilities. Schubert was also present during the formation of Trinity Lutheran Church in Russellville in the fall of 1895. A booklet printed in 1995 celebrating the church's one-hundredth anniversary noted, "John Buchta and Michael Schubert were elected as first deacons." Additionally, Schubert was listed among the first contributors for the new church.

One of Schubert's earliest business endeavors was establishing the Schubert Funeral Service in 1896. Gus Steffens, the son of the Decatur businessman who had taken Schubert under his wing, opened his own funeral home in Russellville several years later. Between his spiritual and business engagements, Schubert again found love and married Emma Kautsch on May 10, 1897. She was of great support when he began to actively expand his businesses.

In 1897, Schubert realized his mercantile building was no longer large enough to accommodate his booming business and added to the brick-faced structure to provide additional space for inventory. For several years, he was a business associate of Frank Weiler and operated under the name Schubert and Weiler Mercantile Company.

"On June 22, 1911, Frank Weiler sold his one-fourth interest in the firm," according to Russellville's sesquicentennial book. "The Schubert Mercantile was lighted by electricity the second week of October 1915. The store now had the appearance of a metropolitan store, having all the modern conveniences such as electric lights, toilets, heat, water, etc."

Left: Losing both his father and mother at a young age, Michael Schubert of Taos became a successful businessman in Russellville. He is pictured in his wedding photo with his second wife, the former Emma Kautsch, in 1897. *Shelly Minton.*

Right: Michael Schubert was seventy-seven years old when he died in 1977. He is interred in Trinity Lutheran Cemetery near Russellville, which he helped establish decades earlier. *Jeremy Ämick.*

Schubert was the father of several children, and his second son, Hugo, entered the mercantile business with his father in 1923. Hugo also continued his father's funeral business and completed embalming school in 1924 to assume management of Schubert Funeral Home. Both the Steffens and Schubert funeral businesses were later purchased by James Scrivner and Jewell Stevinson of Stover.

Michael Schubert, a great visionary of the Russellville community, lived to see Trinity Lutheran Church expand from its small lot on Marion Street to its new brick church, parsonage and small white schoolhouse located on the south side of State Highway C. Following his death on February 17, 1937, the body of the seventy-seven-year-old businessman was laid to rest in the cemetery of Trinity Lutheran Church outside Russellville, which he had helped establish years earlier. Shortly after his death, his widow donated the property upon which the Trinity Lutheran Parish Hall was erected.

Schubert's son Hugo continued to operate the mercantile business until selling it just days before his own death in 1959. The business was later purchased by Arthur Jungmeyer, whose son, Don, utilized the building to operate a grocery store that served the community for many years.

Michael Schubert's contributions to the growth of Russellville cannot easily be described or measured, but a portion of his legacy still remains in his former business building downtown, Trinity Lutheran Church and his home on the southeast corner of Smith and Minnie Streets. It is the legacy of a young man raised in dire circumstances, who sought to immerse himself in the education provided through perseverance and hard work, thus building a loving family and church and rising to the zenith of success in the community he chose as home.

Bailey Lansdown

Iberia Native Became a Respected Businessman in Mid-Missouri Communities

Bailey Lansdown rose from the quiet background of a small town to become an important figure in the early economic stability of several mid-Missouri communities in the early part of the twentieth century. Despite leaving a mark of success wherever he operated a business, he was frequently on the move and focused his sights on achieving his next goal, but never at the expense of honesty and friendship.

In her 1976 book, *The Heritage of Russellville in Cole County*, the late Ruby Koester wrote that Lansdown "was born June 9, 1859 near the town of Iberia. At the age of 21, he started out on his own with $11.65."

The young man may have been somewhat short on operating principal in his early days, but he possessed an unwavering work ethic that was demonstrated during the time he spent shucking corn in Jackson County. Shortly thereafter, he was hired as a hotel clerk in the community of Butler, Missouri. As the years passed, Lansdown appeared to develop both an interest and ability in sales. The *Miller County Autogram-Sentinel* noted in their November 18, 1886 edition that he was employed as a "cigar drummer" (traveling tobacco salesman) for a cigar company out of Kansas City. He was known to frequently visit the mid-Missouri area "looking after the needs of our cigar dealers."

Lansdown entered the mercantile business in the once-bustling towns of Enon, Olean and Decatur, the latter of which is now a ghost town located five miles south of Russellville. While in Decatur, he observed and learned from Frederick Steffens, who owned a successful mill and general store in the community. More importantly, this fortunate association introduced Lansdown to one of Steffens's daughters. On March 21, 1889, he and Theresa (Tracy) Steffens were married at the home of the bride's

NEW Fall Goods

New Shoes	New Overshoes and Boots
" Hats and Caps	New Stoves of all Kinds
" Harness, Collars and Bridles	New Clothing and Overcoats
" Trunks and Suitcases	New Blankets and Comforts
" New Linoleums	New Furnishings and Union Suits
NEW RUGS AT BED ROCK PRICES	
New Ladie's, Misses and Children's Coats	New Dry Goods

Our Prices Are The Lowest---Come In And See

LANSDOWN'S
Money Saving Exchange
Russellville :: :: Missouri

Growing up near Iberia, Bailey Lansdown struck out in life with only $11.65 to his name. He later developed several successful businesses, including a mercantile in Russellville. *Jim and Eve Campbell.*

parents in Decatur. Throughout their many years of marriage, they raised three daughters.

The *Miller County Autogram-Sentinel* glowingly reported on August 12, 1891, that Lansdown was viewed "as one of the finest young men in the state, and we are glad to hear that he is driving a successful business" in Decatur. However, the lure of business opportunities soon inspired his move to another booming town. Russellville was experiencing an unprecedented period of growth, some of which was attributable to what became known as the Bagnell Branch of the Missouri Pacific Railroad, which facilitated the delivery and shipment of assorted commodities. Lansdown migrated to the growing town in 1892, opening a general merchandise store.

Lansdown joined fellow area businessman Michael Schubert in forming the Russellville Exchange Bank in 1895. A few years earlier, Schubert had also been introduced to many successful business practices under the tutelage of Lansdown's father-in-law, Fred Steffens, while living in Decatur. On May 30, 1895, the *Miller County Autogram-Sentinel*, already having published many glowing accounts of Lansdown's accomplishments, reported that the businessman was now supporting the establishment of a newspaper in his adopted community: "Fulton Wilson…informs us that he is making arrangements to begin the publication of a paper at Russellville, Cole County, to be called the Russellville Rustler. He has received good encouragement and among his strongest supporters is our firm merchant friend, Bailey Lansdown, who is conducting an immense business at that place."

History reveals that Lansdown was not alone in recognizing the possibilities unfolding in Russellville since his brother-in-law, Gus Steffens, made the decision to invest in the community when opening the Steffens Funeral Home in 1899. The same year, Lansdown's itinerant nature reemerged, and he sold his business interests in Russellville and moved to nearby Centertown, a bustling small community also served by the railroad. Not only did he open the Lansdown Mercantile Company, but he also became a director in the town's bank and even partnered with Jefferson City interests to work local mines.

According to the *Miller County Autogram-Sentinel* in its January 11, 1912 edition, not only did Lansdown earn the sobriquet of "Merchant Prince of Centertown," but he was also successful at raising livestock and deserved the title of "Cattle King of Cole County."

As the years progressed, Lansdown continued to find success in agricultural endeavors. The *Eldon Advertiser* reported on December 20, 1917, that the successful "cattle man and banker of Centertown" had found yet another profitable investment in raising and selling hogs. In later years, the Lansdown family moved to Jefferson City, remaining active with First Baptist Church. An unyielding businessman, in late 1927, he purchased from his in-laws the Steffens Dry Goods Company in Russellville. Sadly, he did not have the time to develop this business, since he passed away in January 1928. The sixty-eight-year-old was interred in Riverview Cemetery in Jefferson City; his wife, Tracy, passed away in 1966 and lies at rest next to him.

In a period when small newspapers often treated persons of success with a level of apprehension, Lansdown led a clean life that frequently resulted in praise and applause for his varied endeavors. This is evidenced by the stellar remarks written in the *Daily Capital News* on January 21, 1928.

"Few citizens of this section of Central Missouri have been as well and favorably known and held as in high esteem as Mr. Lansdown. He numbered his friends and acquaintances by the thousands and all who came in contact with him in daily life learned to love and admire him for his manly manner, his sterling character, his unquestioned honesty and tireless energy."

The *Russellville Rustler*

For More Than Five Decades, Russellville Newspaper Was Source for Area News

In a period when industry was growing exponentially in Russellville, with such businesses as a lumber yard, roller mill, general stores and a bank to serve the community, there developed the need for an outlet to share stories of local happenings. In 1895, Fulton Wilson chose to pursue this grand endeavor by establishing the first newspaper in Russellville, which would experience multiple owners and survive more than fifty years.

"[Wilson] informs us that he is making arrangements to begin the publication of a paper at Russellville…to be called the Russellville Rustler," shared the *Miller County Autogram-Sentinel* on May 30, 1895. The newspaper boasted that Wilson, then a resident of Eldon, "has the ability to get up a paper that will be a credit to the town."

Wilson, who also pastored at local Christian churches, hired George W. Tremain to fulfill the role of editor for the *Russellville Rustler*. Recognized as a gifted musician, Tremain was an ardent proponent of the community and became a founding member of the Russellville Band, providing musical entertainment at several local events. Tremain soon purchased the newspaper and fulfilled the roles of both owner and editor. In late summer 1899, Marcus T. Tremain of Brussells, Illinois, took over the publication after his brother decided to become a practicing physician and moved to St. Louis.

According to Russellville's sesquicentennial book, after Marcus Tremain purchased the *Rustler* from his brother, he "put in a steam press and a job press. Also, when he took charge, he changed the paper to a four-page home print."

While working to publish a quality newspaper, Marcus Tremain also taught classes for Russellville school and was active in the Modern Woodmen of America (MWA), a fraternal benefit society. He sold the paper in 1903 to take a full-time position of leadership within the MWA.

The *Russellville Rustler* was the first newspaper established in Russellville in 1895, oftentimes operating under different names. For more than fifty years, it provided local subscribers with news of events at the community, state, national and international level. *Jim and Eve Campbell.*

"Editor L.L. Sullins, of the Russellville Rustler, was in Eldon Saturday and gave this office a fraternal call," the *Miller County Autogram-Sentinel* printed in their November 19, 1903 edition. "Mr. Sullins has improved the Rustler in the few months he has had control."

By 1907, B. Ray Franklin had purchased the newspaper, changing the name to *Russellville Weekly Rustler* and seeking to maintain the quality of local reporting that had been its hallmark throughout the years. Not only was the *Rustler* known for sharing local news, but it also printed stories of major national and international consequence.

"Much to the satisfaction of the present management, the Rustler is no longer looked upon by the intelligent people of this section of the state as a mere country newspaper but a county paper that gives the happenings of the county in a fair and impartial way," Franklin printed in the June 7, 1912 edition. "It is no longer looked upon as a charity institution but as a real necessity and many of its readers claim that they would give up all the other papers coming to their address before they would let their favorite paper expire."

Franklin edited and operated the newspaper through 1917, at which time he moved to Jefferson City and became business manager of the *Daily Capital News* and secretary for the Missouri Press Association. He later retired from the newspaper profession and built a resort hotel at the Lake of the Ozarks.

The newspaper operated for the next decade under the name *Central Missouri Leader*, encouraging readers to subscribe at the bargain price of one dollar a year in its edition printed on September 26, 1924.

"Sometime after 1927 and into 1933, the name Rustler seems to have been used again," noted Russellville's sesquicentennial book. "By 1934, the paper had become the *Central Missourian* with W.E. Martin as the editor."

Martin, who had long been associated with the newspaper industry in addition to being involved in several business endeavors, ran the *Central Missourian* for approximately fifteen years, closing it in the late 1940s, thus ending the legacy of a newspaper in Russellville. The building that was home to the original *Russellville Rustler*, located at the corner of Railroad Avenue and Brown Lane, was later torn down, and a garage was erected on the site by the late Ernie Glover. The garage burned several years later, and a newer shop has been built for use by a backhoe service.

There have been attempts to resurrect a newspaper in the community, including the short-lived *Russellville News* in the late 1970s and a more recent newsletter titled the *Russellville Rebel*.

As Eric Partridge reminds us in his book *A Dictionary of Catch Phrases*, famed American humorist Will Rogers once said, "All I know is what I read in the newspapers." No longer do the presses flow freely with ink in the Russellville community. But for more than five decades, subscribers to the various iterations of the local newspaper received their knowledge of activities at the local, state, national and international level through this diminishing format.

George W. Tremain may have become the second owner of the *Russellville Rustler*, but as described in the *Illustrated Sketchbook and Directory of Jefferson City and Cole County*, printed in 1900, his imagination and talents in managing such an enterprise helped elevate the public's perception of the community.

"To Mr. Tremain's four years' residence and enterprising and well directed efforts, greatly aided by his publication, Russellville is largely indebted for her present importance and unusual advantages for a village of its size and environments."

HUNTER & STEVENS LUMBER COMPANY

Former Lumber Company Celebrated 120-Year Legacy in the Russellville Area

During the 1890s, brothers-in-law from Russellville partnered to form a successful lumber company. It was a booming period for the community since there was a railroad spur running through the downtown area, while mercantile companies, funeral homes, blacksmiths and other assorted businesses began erecting storefronts and homes for their families. Andrew A. Hunter "was born on October 21, 1860—near Russellville," noted Reba Koester in the book *The Heritage of Russellville in Cole County*. She added, "He rented a farm in Moniteau County and finally bought one in Russellville, later selling it."

According to *The Illustrated Sketch Book and Directory of Cole County*, on October 2, 1884, Hunter was united in marriage to Callie Stevens, a daughter of businessman Joseph R. Stevens. Hunter was soon acquainted with his wife's younger brother, Ben R. Stevens, and the two became business partners. He and his brother-in-law purchased a lumber company from John Schaeffer situated along the Missouri Pacific Railroad tracks in Russellville, opening the Hunter & Stevens Lumber Company in 1893.

Ben R. Stevens was born one mile south of Russellville in 1868. His mother, the former Elizabeth Enloe, was a direct descendant of Enoch Enloe Sr., a local pioneer who donated the property for Enloe Cemetery in 1866. Stevens married Sadie Hatler, a daughter of local physician Dr. William C. Hatler, in 1891. Supplied in great measure by railroad deliveries, Hunter & Stevens Lumber Yard carried not only lumber but also roofing materials, cement, sand, lime, doors and window sashes. In 1898, under the management of Stevens, they opened a branch of their lumber company in Centertown.

In later years, Hunter was "manager of a lumber yard at Owensville until he disposed of the business and moved to Columbia," reported the *Sunday News and Tribune* on January 3, 1937. The article went on to note that although he remained a co-owner of the lumber yard in Russellville, he had not been active in the business for several years. The growth the Russellville community and the access to material provided by the railroad resulted in a thriving business for Hunter & Stevens for several years. But, like many companies', their purse strings tightened up during the Great Depression and made survival a challenge.

"In talking with a representative of the Hunter and Stevens Lumber Co. Monday, he stated that their business was showing signs of improvement and that many had begun to buy material for remodeling and repairs," reported the *Central Missourian* on October 5, 1933. "Most everyone seems to be looking forward with hopes for better things and better conditions in the future."

A booklet titled *Brief Highlights of the First 100 Years of Russellville Baptist Church*, compiled by Mark Weber, shares that Hunter and his wife were very active in their local congregation. The booklet states that Hunter was a founding member of Russellville Baptist Church in 1903 and helped raise funds for the first church building.

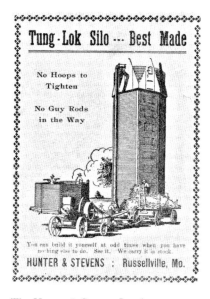

The Hunter & Stevens Lumber Company was established in Russellville in 1893, providing a range of products including silos, such as the one featured in this advertisement from 1916. *Jim and Eve Campbell.*

On January 1, 1937, a seventy-six-year-old Hunter passed away at his home in Maplewood, Missouri. His remains were returned to his hometown and interred in Enloe Cemetery, where his parents and many of his in-laws had been laid to rest.

Ben Stevens maintained an active interest not only in the lumber business but in community affairs and organizations as well. For many years, he served as a member of the board of trustees of Enloe Cemetery and, in 1937, was appointed by Governor Stark to the Democratic Central Committee from Cole County. The year of 1944 marked a dark period for Stevens, since his wife passed away at seventy years of age, followed by his decision to sell his business in Russellville to Scruggs-Guhleman Lumber Company. Four years later, he passed away and was laid to rest next to his wife in Enloe Cemetery.

Marvin Jungmeyer, a Russellville native, was eleven or twelve years old when he began his first job in town making egg crates for the local MFA. Several years later, in 1947, he was hired to work for Scruggs-Guhleman.

"I worked there in the afternoons after school and during the summer months," Jungmeyer recalled. "I did all kinds of odd jobs around there.…I didn't really have any kind of special title," he chuckled.

Graduating from Russellville High School in 1950, he continued working at the lumber company. In 1953, he married Margaret Carol Mahan, the granddaughter of Ben Stevens, one of the original founders of the Hunter & Stevens Lumber Company.

"I was in the U.S. Army from 1953 to 1955, did my basic training at Fort Riley, Kansas, and later served with the infantry at Fort Carson, Colorado," Jungmeyer recalled.

Russellville native Ben R. Stevens cofounded the Hunter & Stevens Lumber Company. Decades later, it was purchased by Marvin Jungmeyer, who operated it as Jungmeyer Lumber Company until 2013. *Sonny Jungmeyer.*

After receiving his discharge, Jungmeyer returned to work for the Scruggs-Guhleman Lumber Company in Russellville. However, a few years after one of the company's founders, Cliff Scruggs, passed away, Jungmeyer purchased the lumber company in Russellville, changing the name to Jungmeyer Lumber Company. The lumber business remained a vital part of the community until 2013, at which time he decided to close the company.

"I had reached eighty years old and felt like I was getting old enough to retire," Jungmeyer said.

One of the most rewarding aspects of his career in the lumber industry, Jungmeyer maintained, was not only being part of a 120-year family legacy but also all of the wonderful people he met along the way.

"The lumber business was a great experience and was always very good to me," he said. "One of the best parts of it happened to be all of the great customers that I worked with—they made it all worthwhile."

KAUTSCH AND LINHARDT

A.N. Linhardt Built Upon Early Mercantile Foundations Established in Lohman

Many rural communities can trace their once-bustling mercantile operations to certain individuals who used their knowledge and drive to build businesses that survived the decades. The late Adam Nicholas (A.N.) Linhardt was one such visionary, whose early desire to seek an alternative to farming resulted in a respected mercantile in Lohman that built upon the foundations of a previous business and later expanded to Jefferson City.

Born near Lohman in 1883, Linhardt was only thirteen years old when his father was murdered in town, leaving many members of the community reeling in shock. Although the culprit was caught and hanged for the crime, young Linhardt and his family could not indulge in grief since they needed to make a living in the small railroad community.

Natalie Young, granddaughter of A.N. Linhardt, recalled, "My Grandfather Linhardt was a man of smaller stature and said, 'I was the runt of the family.' He believed that he was not cut out to be a farmer and had to decide what type of work suited him. He started with clerk jobs in general stores."

For six years, Linhardt was employed as a clerk at Kautsch and Linhardt, a mercantile established in 1887, which was initially housed in a brick building

A.N. Linhardt (*third from left*) is pictured in front of his successful mercantile company in Lohman in 1915. The mercantile was directly across the street from the brick building that served as the first Linhardt and Kautsch general store. *Gert Strobel.*

formerly used by Farmers Bank of Lohman. The business was co-owned by his first cousin, John Adam Linhardt, who operated in partnership with John Henry Kautsch, a former business associate of the town's namesake, Charles W. Lohman. The store sold all sorts of general merchandise, in addition to farm equipment such as binders and mowers, to residents of the community and surrounding areas. Sales were also boosted by foot traffic since the store was located only a short walk from Missouri Pacific Railroad depot, a hotel and saloon.

"Around 1908–1909, they moved across the street and constructed the fine building on the west side of Main Street," noted *A Bicentennial View*—a historical booklet about Lohman printed in 1976. "Mr. Ed Baumann was a partner in this firm after the turn of the century," the booklet added.

The *Sunday News and Tribune* reported in their December 8, 1935 edition that Linhardt left his clerk position at Kautsch and Linhardt and, for two years, operated a lumber yard in Lohman. His future plans continued to unfold in 1910, when he married Anna Schoch of Russellville. Soon, an important decision needed to be made regarding where the couple would reside.

"My grandfather asked his wife if she preferred to live in Lohman or Jefferson City, as they would surely make their home near his work," said Natalie Young. "My grandmother Anna told me that she said she liked Lohman but felt the final decision had to be his."

A.N. Linhardt chose Lohman, where he set down roots by building a home. In 1911, the year following his marriage, he had made enough of a profit from his work in the lumber business to purchase the firm of Kautsch and Linhardt. He later shared that after purchasing the business, he went on the roof of the store building and painted over the name Kautsch on the sign. Linhardt was joined in partnership by Walter Fischer in 1912, but in 1917, he became the sole proprietor of the store.

"Along with the general store, there was a farm implement area on the south side of the store," said Natalie Young. "As motorized farm equipment was developing at that time, Grandpa Nick both sold and repaired the equipment. He reminisced that when he ordered merchandise by the train car load, it was good for the Lohman economy."

The Linhardts became parents to five sons and a daughter; one daughter died in infancy. Three of their sons later assisted in Linhardt's business endeavors, including the opening of A.N. Linhardt and Sons in Jefferson City in 1936. The store, located on Mulberry Street, sold the complete line of McCormick and Deering farm machines and implements. Linhardt, his

John Adam Linhardt and John Henry Kautsch established their first mercantile in Lohman in 1887. The business was initially housed in a brick building most recently used by the Farmers Bank of Lohman. *Gert Strobel.*

son Harley and a store employee suffered serious injury in October 1936, when a barrel of tar they were heating with a blowtorch exploded in the back of their store in Jefferson City. Boiling tar scalded the faces of all three men, who were transported to St. Mary's Hospital by the fire department.

Natalie Young recalled, "Uncle Harley was treated by one doctor, and the tar and debris were removed so he could heal. Grandpa got a different doctor, and he just bandaged him. Uncle Harley started healing, but grandpa did not. A nurse privately spoke with grandma and said if they didn't change doctors, grandpa would surely die. Grandma made the decision to change doctors, and grandpa's wounds were cleaned, and he survived to old age."

The store in Lohman remained in operation until 1942, but Linhardt continued his farm implement dealership in Jefferson City for several years. He would also go on to serve as president of the Farmers Bank of Lohman from 1955 to 1961. His wife, Anna, lived to be eighty-six years old and passed away in 1976. Ten years later, at the impressive age of 103, Linhardt died and was laid to rest next to his wife in the cemetery of St. Paul's Lutheran Church in Lohman.

Businesses have come and gone in many a small town, but occasionally the storefronts erected have survived the unyielding passage of time, boldly standing in silent tribute to the entrepreneurs who once developed grand plans and clung to lofty dreams. In the small community of Lohman, the names of Kautsch and Linhardt are still present in descendants living throughout the community. And although A.N. Linhardt may not be widely remembered among current residents, evidence of the booming local economy he and his predecessors once helped create continues through stalwart buildings proudly flanking Main Street.

The Russellville Hotel

Built in 1897, Former Russellville Hotel
Remains a Community Fixture

The former Russellville Hotel was a thriving venture with a story that began to unfold in 1897, during a period of unprecedented growth in the downtown area. Facing the tracks of the old Missouri Pacific Railroad, the hotel was an establishment that came to fruition through the efforts of individuals who possessed a shared heritage of immigrant parents in addition to family connections resulting from marriage.

Louis Schneider was the first owner of the Russellville Hotel, built in 1897 and opened the following year in partnership with his older brother, George. The historic building is still in use as a bar and apartments. *Jim and Eve Campbell.*

Born on a farm near Taos on May 15, 1869, Louis Schneider attended area schools and was taught at an early age the value of hard work under the guidance of his parents, both of whom were German immigrants.

"[Louis Schneider] engaged in farming until 1897, when he sold out and moved to Russellville," wrote Reba Koester in *The Heritage of Russellville in Cole County*. "He built a two-story brick building, 56 x 86 ft., that housed the most comfortable and inviting hotel in the county at that time."

The hotel opened on April 2, 1898, and collected $200 in receipts on its first day of business. Additionally, as Russellville's sesquicentennial book described, "In connection with the hotel was a well-appointed bar, supplied with everything that could be demanded by the most exacting taste in the way of wines, brandies, beer, etc."

The hotel was designed by Charles Opel, a renowned architect and builder from Jefferson City who was associated with many impressive structures throughout the state, including several that are in the National Register of

Historic Places. Schneider's new hotel was located in a connected row of downtown buildings adjacent to a mercantile business owned by Michael Schubert, the son of German immigrants and a fellow native of Taos. On March 13, 1887, Louis Schneider's brother, George, married Schubert's younger sister, Katherine.

"[George Schneider] engaged in farming near Shipley Shoals for five years, when he purchased the farm he still owns near Brazito," noted *The Illustrated Sketchbook and Directory of Jefferson City and Cole County*. The book added, "He associated with his brother, Louis, in the hotel business at Russellville in April 1898, where he now makes his home, still retaining his farm, which he rents."

Louis soon met and was engaged to Katherine Sinish of Russellville. The couple married on July 4, 1899, at a time when the hotel and saloon businesses were beginning to transition into a lucrative endeavor.

Many small towns of the era came to accept the vices associated with the sale of alcohol and the presence of saloons as a common reality of the railroad, but in Russellville, temperance-minded individuals created much dismay for the Schneider brothers even years prior to Prohibition. The *Russellville Rustler* newspaper reported on October 23, 1908, "John L. Chambers, John A. Hunter, William and True DeFoe and T.A. Shepherd, residents of Russellville, have filed a petition in the circuit court against George and Louis Schneider.…The object of this suit is to try and revoke the license and make Russellville a dry town."

Oral history passed down by local residents maintains that Silas Jasper Howard, who operated a blacksmith shop in the community, was an avowed prohibitionist. If he needed to pass by the saloon, he would stroll a short distance into the street rather than walk directly in front of the building.

Reba Koester wrote about the eventual success of those opposing the sale of alcohol in *The Heritage of Russellville in Cole County*, noting, "Some of you will recall Russellville Hotel closed its doors to business when the saloon had to close in February 1914.…George Schneider bought the entire building from his brother and opened the hotel again."

Alcohol sales were again permitted in the community in 1918. However, in 1920, sales were suspended following the enactment of the Eighteenth Amendment to the Constitution, which remained in place for the next thirteen years and became known as Prohibition.

In the years after George Schneider purchased the building from his brother, a section of the first floor of the building adjacent to the saloon became a barbershop operated by his son-in-law, Fred Dampf.

Louis Schneider was fifty-two years old when he died in 1921, six years after selling the hotel to his older brother. He was laid to rest in Riverview Cemetery in Jefferson City, followed by the burial of his wife thirty-two years later. The hotel continued to operate throughout the ensuing years, often under different ownership. In October 1924, the Russellville Hotel was leased by Mrs. A.E. Hake of Mary's Home and not only boasted first-class accommodations but also offered lunch and dinner for shoppers and farmers trading in the community.

In the late 1920s, the building was purchased by Gus Steffens, who utilized the saloon section for his undertaking business while maintaining the hotel section to provide accommodations for travelers and guests. George Schneider remained in the Russellville area for the remainder of his days, passing away on February 14, 1944, at the advanced age of eighty-six. He was buried in Trinity Lutheran Cemetery near Russellville with his wife, who had passed away eighteen years earlier.

Long gone are the days when the Russellville Hotel hosted travelers; instead, the upper level has been converted into apartments. The saloon has also weathered the decades, remaining a bar that has existed under a host of different owners. There may have been untold quantities of beer spilled on the old hardwood floor of the saloon, and the steps to the hotel may be well trodden by travelers, but it is an edifice that has endured for more than a century and offers the community many additional years of use.

As English writer John Ruskin explained, many such buildings can be considered gifts from our predecessors. "When we build, let us think that we build forever," he wrote. "Let it not be for present delight nor for present use alone. Let it be such work as our descendants will thank us for."

RUSSELLVILLE ROLLER MILLS

A Successful Business Endeavor of Jacob L. Ritchie

The railroad brought an economic boom to Russellville in the late nineteenth century, leading to the development and expansion of several business ventures. But as the population around the community continued to grow, the need was recognized for a roller mill that could process locally produced grain into flour, inspiring the town to make a generous offer to a farmer.

"Jacob Lee Ritchie, one of the proprietors of the Russellville Roller Mills, was born on a farm near Prairie Home [on] June 21, 1864," noted the late

Erna Raithel in Russellville's sesquicentennial book. "For four years, he rented a farm near his birthplace; he also had a threshing machine and a sawmill."

Ritchie demonstrated his proclivity for expanding upon his agricultural interests by purchasing a farm in Moniteau County and eventually partnering with C.A. Edwards to build a mill in the small Boone County community of Huntsdale, where they began processing winter wheat into flour. The Russellville area acquired the reputation of producing quality wheat, but since there was not a roller mill in town, local farmers made trips to locations such as the Flessa Flouring Mills in Centertown or the mill in nearby Decatur (a now-defunct community south of Russellville) to have their wheat processed.

In an effort to develop the local economy and assist farmers with processing their wheat crops, business owners raised $1,000, offering it to Ritchie, along with a free piece of property, if he built a roller mill in Russellville.

"He accepted the proposition and built a fifty-barrel roller mill," the sesquicentennial book revealed. "It soon became necessary for him to increase the capacity of the mill."

The late L.A.B. Leslie, former Russellville postmaster and historian, wrote, "The water to run the mill was supplied by a large pond that was the delight of all the young people in that ice skating was allowed."

The mill was located on a piece of property on the corner of Jefferson and Marion Streets, a short distance from the railroad. In attendance for the dedication, occurring around 1900, were several well-known local business owners. Michael Schubert, owner of a successful Russellville mercantile, and Frederick Steffens, who owned a roller mill in Decatur, were present for the event. Ritchie soon brought in Russellville area native and farmer William Allen Stark as a partner, and they quickly doubled the capacity of the mill. Stark had garnered a reputation as a gifted carpenter and built a stunning home below the mill that became the residence for Ritchie and his growing family.

In 1904, exhibiting restlessness and continued zeal for exploring other business opportunities, Ritchie and Stark sold the mill to August Sauer, who not only handled wheat but also sold different types of meal and feed. For a short time, Sauer operated the mill in partnership with Herman Brunning, before assuming full ownership. After selling the mill, Ritchie and his family moved to Eugene, where he opened the community's first flour mill and later purchased an interest in the Eugene Mercantile Company.

Above: The dedication of the Russellville Roller Mills is pictured circa 1900, under the ownership of Jacob Lee Ritchie. The business was embraced by local farmers, whose wheat was milled into fine flour. *Jim and Eve Campbell.*

Right: August Sauer, the second owner of the Russellville Roller Mills, advertised his business in booklets printed for the Russellville Street Fairs held in the early 1900s. *Jim and Eve Campbell.*

RUSSELLVILLE ROLLER

MILLS

Russellville, Missouri

AUGUST SAUER, Prop.

High Grade Flours, Meal and all kinds of Grain and Feed. Highest market price paid at all times for Wheat, Corn and Grain. Farmers and merchants will find it to their interest to patronize us.

Good Service and Fair Dealing

"August Sauer, at the Russellville Mill, has had a very busy week buying and handling wheat," reported the *Russellville Rustler* on August 13, 1909. "There has been a constant string of wagons at his place and he has something like 3,000 bushels of wheat on hand at the mill."

In July 1914, Sauer dispelled the false rumor that he had sold the mill and encouraged farmers to continue bringing their wheat. Throughout the next several years, shares of interest in the mill were purchased by Andy and Martin Doehla, both of whom were involved with the mill in nearby Lohman. In 1919, recognizing the need for better access to the railroad for shipment of their products, they constructed a scale near the depot, according to *The Heritage of Russellville in Cole County*.

The *Cole County Weekly Rustler* reported on July 2, 1926, that the mill had been targeted by criminals. "The burglars gained entrance to the building by smashing a front window. Unable to open the large cash register, they carried it away with them to the old Boaz mines where it was open[ed] and looted and then abandoned."

Sales of flour to the Missouri State Penitentiary provided additional economic stability for the mill. Sadly, primary owner August Sauer was killed in a truck accident near Tipton in August 1929; his shares in the mill transferred to Andy and Mike Doehla. A drought in the early 1930s decimated a large swath of wheat crops throughout the Midwest and, combined with the financial distresses of the Great Depression, led to the mill being closed in 1933.

John F. Morrow, a building contractor from Russellville, disassembled the mill in the years after the Great Depression. The pond needed to provide water for the steam engines used in milling was later drained and filled with dirt. The final removal of the mill's existence came in April 2003, when the home built for the mill's founder, Jacob Ritchie, burned to the ground.

Ritchie was a man of foresight and vision, grasping an opportunity to develop the initially successful business that became the Russellville Roller Mills. The *Illustrated Sketchbook and Directory of Jefferson City and Cole County* stated that he displayed a rare mixture of skills that helped a young man leaving home with only $150 garner a reputation for commercial achievement. "Mr. Ritchie is a self-made man who is a natural mechanic. His knowledge of machinery and mechanism and his practical ability to construct is rarely found in a man with practical business sense and untiring industry."

Scrivner-Smith-Morrow Mercantile

Former Mercantile in Russellville Represented Family Connections

Russellville was experiencing a robust commercial environment during the early 1900s. The town boasted a hotel, saloon, doctors, stores and other assorted companies, all of which benefited from the traffic of the Missouri Pacific Railroad branch. The year of 1908 evolved into a record moment for the community with the beginnings of the Russellville Street Fair and the establishment of a mercantile that represented a partnership between several local business visionaries. The *National Corporation Report* stated in its Volume 36, covering the period of February 20, 1908, to August 13, 1908, that Scrivner-Smith-Morrow Mercantile Company incorporated in Russellville with $10,000. The business was listed as a partnership between "L.A. Scrivner, F. Steffens, P.D. Smith, J.J. Morrow [and] B.W. Lansdown."

The Scrivner-Smith-Morrow Mercantile opened in Russellville in 1908, near the Missouri Pacific Railroad depot. The company benefited from the investment of successful business owners such as Fritz Steffens and Ben Lansdown. *Jim and Eve Campbell.*

Early success of the new endeavor was likely with Fritz Steffens as a shareholder; he was a German immigrant who had served as postmaster in the former community of Decatur while operating a successful roller mill there. At the time the new mercantile opened, Steffens's son, Gus, owned a funeral home in Russellville. Bailey Lansdown, a fellow shareholder in the new Scrivner-Smith-Morrow Mercantile, received business training under Fritz Steffens and later married one of his daughters. Years earlier, Lansdown opened a mercantile in Russellville, but by 1908, he had moved his business operations to the community of Centertown.

A two-story brick building was erected in 1908 across from the train depot in downtown Russellville, on the corner of Railroad Avenue and McDavitt Street. The new Scrivner-Smith-Morrow Mercantile sat next to the home and office of Dr. Walter Leslie, "a practicing family physician for over 50 years in the…community," according to Russellville's sesquicentennial book.

The opening year for the new business was boosted by an emerging local event that would, for the next several years, bring business to the new mercantile from locations throughout the region: the Russellville Street Fair.

"Russellville certainly has done herself proud during the fair and it was the biggest advertisement the town ever had," reported the *Russellville Rustler* on September 18, 1908. "Russellville people never do things by halves and if everybody will lend a helping hand next year, we can have the best fair in Central Missouri." The newspaper also reported that in midsummer of the following year, a burglar broke into one of the rear windows of the store and escaped with a nine-dollar watch, several pocketknives and some smoking tobacco.

Period advertisements reveal the store, like so many stores of the era, offered the community an intriguing range of products, including footwear, caskets, farm implements, dry goods and groceries, the latter of which included fresh produce purchased from local farmers and growers.

Lairie Anderson Scrivner, born in the near-forgotten community of Scrivner, south of Russellville, was a founding investor in the mercantile and had gained experience managing a general store in the community. By 1912, he sold his interest in the company and moved to the community of Fort Collins, Colorado, where, in 1924, he opened Scrivner's Grocery and Market.

Shares in the mercantile transferred between different investors several times throughout the next few years. Henry E. Steffens, son of founding shareholder Fritz Steffens, was eventually brought into the company fold.

"A deal was complete Tuesday of this week, whereby H.E. Steffens, living near Brazito, became the owner of fifteen shares of stock of the Scrivner-

Smith-Morrow Merc. Co. of Russellville, which he purchased from his father," wrote the *Russellville Rustler* on October 9, 1914.

During this time frame, improvements were made to the mercantile, resulting in the addition of a new grocery counter and a significant remodeling of the interior. Additionally, rolling ladders were installed in the dry goods and shoe departments, making it easier to access items that were stored on shelves.

"W.R. Hodge of California, formerly in mercantile business in Elston and Centertown, has purchased stock in the Scrivner-Smith-Morrow Mercantile Company of Russellville and will become its manager immediately," reported the *Eldon Advertiser* on November 18, 1915.

Despite investment from outside the community, local family connections remained strong within the company. Mamie Dampf—daughter of George Schneider, the co-owner of the Russellville Hotel and Saloon—was previously employed as a clerk in the mercantile and later purchased John Jasper Morrow's stock for $4,235. Mamie's husband, Fred Dampf, operated a barbershop for many years in a section of the building next to the saloon owned by his father-in-law. Michael Schubert, Mamie's uncle, was also a successful business owner, operating Schubert's Mercantile Company a short distance to the east.

The Russellville Fair, which had for several years brought business to the community, came to an end in 1914. The Scrivner-Smith-Morrow Mercantile Company continued to survive the next few years, but a triad of dire circumstances, all within the same year, inspired its eventual conclusion.

Passenger service along the Bagnell Branch of the Missouri Pacific Railroad ceased in 1932, resulting in fewer people traveling by rail through the town. The same year, fire completely destroyed the mercantile building during a period of bucket brigades and prior to the organization of a fire department. Finally, in the summer of 1932, the stock markets fell to their lowest point of the Great Depression, becoming the final nail in the coffin for the once-robust business.

Improvements were made to the mercantile, resulting in a new grocery counter and significant remodeling of the interior. This newspaper advertisement shows some of the varied products offered at the store. *Jim and Eve Campbell.*

The Scrivner-Smith-Morrow Mercantile was, for many years, a bustling center of economic activity in the Russellville community; now, nothing denotes its existence other than a flat, grassy lot across from Community Point Bank. Memories oftentimes outlive buildings, and the storied past of the mercantile provides a glimpse into the business associations of a number of local residents and their families, all of whom toiled to build and strengthen their community while providing for a decent future for their families and loved ones.

John R. Strobel

Operated a Unique Mercantile Business in Lohman Community

The early history of Lohman features the establishment of the Soell & Plochberger Mercantile, which was situated on lots once owned by Charles W. Lohman, for whom the town was named. This business remained for many years a partnership between Christian Soell—a German immigrant—and his younger brother-in-law, Otto Plochberger. These merchants became well known throughout the local area for the assortment of products they stocked.

In 1947, the property was sold to John R. "J.R." Strobel and his wife, Lucille. Strobel was a forty-five-year-old local farmer who made a family affair out of opening and operating the John R. Strobel General Merchandise Store, which was located on Front Street across from the railroad depot in Lohman.

"Everything from the old-fashioned square wrought iron nails to a John Deere tractor," boasted Strobel of his product variety in an advertisement from 1953. The ad further revealed that the store's $20,000 in stock also included groceries, hardware, dry goods and novelties.

This period also brought about a difficult moment in the new store's history. J.R. Strobel announced a closeout sale in 1953, which would afford him the opportunity to dedicate more time to responsibilities on the farm while also attempting to heal from recent injuries.

"At one time, dad was hurt when a truck backed into him, and he was caught between a barn door and the vehicle," said his daughter, Ruth Strobel. "I was really little, but I remember him being in the hospital for quite some time."

The Soell and Plochberger Mercantile was purchased by J.R. Strobel in 1947. The building and adjacent house still stand in Lohman. *Jim and Eve Campbell.*

The store was able to survive through the help of Strobel's family, who worked to ensure the needs of local customers were met. This combined effort not only included the long hours worked by Strobel's wife, Lucille, but also the support of her brother, Paul McDaniel.

"I was born in 1952, and we lived on a farm outside of Lohman until November 1956," recalled Dennis Strobel, J.R.'s son. "That's when we moved into the house next to the store, and [that] is where my brother and our three sisters grew up." He added, "That's also when our mother started working in the store a lot more."

Virtually everything Dennis and his family needed came from the store. As he recalled, in addition to the products listed in the aforementioned newspaper ad, they also sold such products as Wolverine shoes, ammunition, bolts of cloth, beans in bulk and, oddly enough, dynamite.

Ruth Strobel noted, "There were times that I would ride down to Richland [Missouri] with Dad to pick up a load of dynamite. We not only sold it and the blasting caps to local farmers but to the county road department for some of their construction projects. It was stored in a shed behind the store."

Dennis recalled, "I started working in the store when I was around eight years old and remember roller skating on the second floor of the building. There was stuff in there that was left over from Soell & Plochberger's store, like bars of old soap, washing powder and horse collars."

In front of the building, his father catered to local motorists by having two gas pumps installed. Further supplementing his extensive and diverse selection of merchandise, Strobel also carried a selection of oils, fan belts, farm implements, cigarettes and chewing tobacco.

"You could say it really was a one-stop shop for just about everything you would ever need," Dennis chuckled. "There was kerosene for sale, and at lunchtime we sliced meat and made sandwiches. A lot of the employees from the old Lohman mill and the Lohman Exchange, along with local farmers, would stop in and get something to eat."

Ruth added, "One thing I remember is that the priest would come over from the St. Martins parish and purchase their communion wine from the store."

In the back of the store, there was a large safe concreted into the floor. Upon it was inscribed the name of the town's namesake, Charles W. Lohman.

"That was really an interesting piece of local history," said Dennis.

As the years passed, the children of J.R. and Lucille moved away to embark upon their adult lives. In the late 1970s, with business declining, J.R. and his wife made the decision to sell the store, and the contents were auctioned off in 1979. The couple spent their remaining years living in Jefferson City, where J.R. passed away in 1991. Lucille succeeded him in death five years later and lies at rest next to her husband in the cemetery of St. John's Lutheran Church in Stringtown.

John R. Strobel opened the J.R. General Merchandise Store in Lohman in 1947. Prior to its closure in the late 1970s, it sold products including gasoline, groceries, tobacco, dry goods, ammunition, farm implements and dynamite. *Jim and Eve Campbell.*

Strobel's children reflected that although the store sold most goods needed by those in the surrounding community, it suffered the reality of many forgotten businesses of the past. It is now an empty building long since closed for business because of the changing economic circumstances affecting many small towns.

"It seemed like Dad spent a good part of his life worrying about paying his bills while also trying to make sure the store had everything people would want or need," said Dennis Strobel. "When he finally sold the store, it was like a great weight had been lifted from his shoulders." He added, "Before the store shut its doors, I recall Dad saying that Lohman had become less of a farming community and turned into more of a bedroom community for Jefferson City. He recognized that people were working in Jefferson City and making most of their purchases there, and that spelled the end for the business. But working there with my family was a great education, and perhaps one I didn't fully appreciate at the time."

KARR THEATER

Clarence T. Karr Brought Motion Pictures to Russellville in the Early 1920s

Clarence "C.T." Karr was a man who gazed into the future, recognizing an opportunity to bring motion pictures to Russellville in the early 1920s. His experience in the electrical industry combined with his business savvy ensured that residents of the community could enjoy the cinema—a privilege often only available in larger cities—while also witnessing the technological transition from silent films with subtitles to those with sound.

Born near Henley on February 26, 1899, Karr was raised the son of a well driller. As he came of age, he was self-employed as an automobile mechanic in Eugene, gaining a bevy of expertise that would benefit him greatly as he began to map out his future.

During World War I, Karr continued his automotive work since he was not yet twenty-one years old nor required to register for the draft. On September 12, 1918, with the minimum age being lowered to eighteen, the nineteen-year-old Karr registered with his local draft board but was never called to service, since the armistice was signed weeks later.

"(Clarence) Karr is the new manager of the Eugene Theater and had tickets printed [while visiting Tuscumbia]," reported the *Miller Country Autogram-Sentinel* on June 2, 1921.

The newspaper noted that Karr and his business associate, Ben Hodge, purchased a building in Eugene and operated "the picture show in connection with an electric plant and battery charging station." Two years later, Karr embarked upon another endeavor when resolving to forgo his business aspirations in Eugene and open a theater in a nearby growing community in partnership with his father.

The *Central Missouri Leader* reported in the February 16, 1923 edition that "J.W. Karr and son…have purchased the old Christian Church building at this place and are this week remodeling same and installing motion picture machinery and expect to start a high-grade motion picture show in Russellville."

The community's only newspaper of the period, the *Russellville Rustler*, strongly encouraged those in the community to support the new endeavor. In a column dated February 23, 1923, a reporter wrote, "Russellville is to have a moving picture show which will open Saturday night, Feb. 24th. A good show should have the patronage of the community. Keep the enterprise going."

Located in the alley on Grace Street on the south side of Russellville Baptist Church, the theater building underwent a significant renovation with Karr and his father sparing little expense in making it a comfortable and welcome attraction.

"Everyone enjoyed the movie show, which made its opening here Saturday night," reported the *Russellville Rustler* on March 2, 1923. "There will be a show twice a week, Wednesday and Saturday night of each week, meeting a long felt need for something in way of amusement in Russellville."

Through welcome foresight, Karr not only brought a fascinating technology to throngs of receptive moviegoers in a rural community but also helped introduce a new viewing opportunity.

An article by Erin McDowell titled "The Rise and Fall of Movie Theaters," appearing in *Business Insider* on May 26, 2020, explained, "Films with sound were added in 1927, which opened up the movie going experience to a much wider audience. Cinema visitors no longer had to be literate to enjoy a film."

Business activities notwithstanding, perhaps the most remarkable of his new engagements in Russellville came when he met Marie Campbell, whom he married on October 30, 1925.

Electricity had been available in the community for several years yet was generally only affordable to business owners. Opportunity came knocking once again for Karr in 1929 with the arrival of rural electrification brought by Missouri Power & Light Company.

"C.T. Karr is busy wiring the Dr. Glover residence preparatory to installing the lighting fixtures," reported the *Jefferson City Post-Tribune* on July 25, 1929. "Mr. Karr has proven himself capable of good work in this line of electrical services and has done a large percentage of the house-wiring in Russellville."

The theater became a location to host a variety of events outside of motion pictures, such as school plays, banquets, meetings for local farm organizations and performances by popular area string bands. Regrettably, its demise and eventual closure came during the heart of the Great Depression. Some years later, the theater was demolished and Russellville Baptist Church has since

C.T. Karr is pictured in Russellville in the early 1960s with his wife, Marie. In the background is their former business, Karr Hardware. Karr erected an outdoor theater, a follow-up to the indoor theater he and his father brought to town in 1923. *Jim and Eve Campbell.*

built a four-door garage on the site. Karr went on to purchase the building that once housed the Farmers and Merchants Bank, opening a new business, Karr Hardware. Intriguingly, this new venture did not signal the end of motion pictures in town.

"Russellville is to have a local move theater," printed the *Daily Capital News* on May 24, 1947. "C.T. Karr has made arrangements to hold open air shows at the rear of the hardware store. Mr. Karr has new show equipment of the latest type and intends to give the town and community a better class of pictures."

The open-air theater became a fun and memorable attraction for the area. Although Karr and his wife never had children of their own, they found great satisfaction in seeing those in the community enjoying movies with their parents.

Clarence Karr passed away in 1973 and lies at rest alongside his wife in Enloe Cemetery near Russellville.

"Those who don't believe in magic will never find it," wrote children's author Roald Dahl. For years, the eyes of youth from Russellville and outlying rural areas gazed with wonderment upon a movie screen provided by an individual possessing a love of cinema. The enchanted moments of evenings spent outdoors among neighbors and family, along with the scent of fresh popcorn sweetening the air, have become treasured memories fortifying the legacy of the late C.T. Karr.

Arthur Jungmeyer

Well-Known Contractor
Helped Build the Russellville Community

Born in 1906 on a farm in rural Cole County, Arthur Jungmeyer came from a pioneering family of German immigrants who helped establish St. Paul's Lutheran Church in Lohman. In his early years, he attended classes at both Lohman School and the German school at St. Paul's before eventually settling in a nearby community, where he would help contribute to economic growth.

"In 1908, Dad [Wilhelm] bought the lumber yard in Lohman, sold it in 1912 and moved to a farm near Russellville," Arthur Jungmeyer recorded several decades ago in handwritten notes. He added, "I started Van Pool School District in 1912, and in the fall of 1918, moved on the farm near Lohman where my great grandpa from Germany settled in 1836."

A newsletter from Villa Marie (the nursing facility where Jungmeyer would later reside) noted, "At age 14, [Arthur] was recognized by the Bagnell Branch [Missouri Pacific Railroad] for extinguishing a fire on a railroad bridge close to the family farm. He was awarded $5.00 from the Railroad Company, which in 1920 was a handsome reward."

After working on his family's farm, the next major step in Jungmeyer's employment came when he was hired at the Lohman Producer's Exchange in 1923, when he was only seventeen years old. Soon, he met the woman with whom he would spend the next several decades.

"He was married in 1928 to Ruth Goldammer," wrote L.A.B. Leslie in an early 1970s article. "They have two sons and two daughters."

Russellville's sesquicentennial book stated, "In September 1929, the Board of Directors for the MFA Oil Company authorized the purchase of Standard Oil at Russellville for $200. The bulk plant, one of the original 25 of MFA Oil, opened for business in January 1930, with Arthur Jungmeyer as manager."

For nearly the next decade, Jungmeyer remained employed with MFA Oil as a wholesale distributor, making deliveries of assorted petroleum products throughout the area. The following years brought an assortment of employment opportunities for Jungmeyer; he went to work for the MFA Exchange and the Jefferson City Baking Company and finally entered the building trades. During World War II, he worked construction projects at locations including Fort Leonard Wood and Scott Field, Illinois.

After the war, Jungmeyer fulfilled the role of city marshal for the community of Russellville. In 1947, city records reveal that he ticketed a local resident for "drinking and swearing." The defendant appeared before the town board and, for his violation, was fined $7.50.

Leveraging the training he received while working government construction projects, "in 1952, he began his own business as a building contractor, building 97 homes and various other buildings in Jefferson City, Russellville and throughout the surrounding areas," according to his obituary. One of the highlights of his contracting work included the development of the "Jungmeyer Addition," a community of homes he built

Arthur Jungmeyer was a construction contractor in the Russellville area who became involved in the growth of the community. In 1928, he married Ruth Goldammer in Lohman. *Jim and Eve Campbell.*

west of the Russellville City Park and elementary school. His obituary added, "[He] was a very strong supporter of growth and betterment of the community."

His community-mindedness was not only represented by his commercial endeavors but also by his participation in other volunteer activities around Russellville. Jungmeyer and his family were active members of Trinity Lutheran Church, where he served on different boards and committees. In addition to serving as an alderman with the city council of Russellville, he was also instrumental in the founding of the Russellville Lions Club, becoming a charter member on November 22, 1949. For decades, he supported the club as they sponsored many community improvements such as the development of the local water works and the volunteer fire department.

"Arthur Jungmeyer, a local contractor, has purchased the building which housed the Schubert Mercantile Company," reported the *California Democrat* on February 22, 1962. "He plans to repair and remodel the building."

The building, which dates back to the late 1890s, was soon remodeled and later held the offices of an insurance company, a local physician and different stores. In December 1984, one of Jungmeyer's sons, Don, opened Jungmeyer's Grocery in the former mercantile building. Another of Jungmeyer's four children, Marvin, engaged in his own business endeavors, operating for several decades the Jungmeyer Lumber Company in Russellville.

Ever the visionary and constantly seeking ways to improve his community, Jungmeyer served on the board of the Russellville Senior Housing Association. The outcome of this effort was the construction of sixteen units of affordable senior housing, located on a five-acre tract on the east side of town.

"Ruth had a severe stroke [on] September 25th 1992 and died October 23rd, 1992," Jungmeyer wrote of his wife in later years. "We were married 64 years on that day. How we miss her every day."

Following the death of his beloved wife, Jungmeyer continued living in Russellville until age and infirmity necessitated his move to an assisted living facility. Frequently stating his desire to live to be one hundred years old, he passed away on May 6, 2006, nearly two months prior to achieving this goal. He was laid to rest alongside his wife in the Trinity Lutheran Church Cemetery near Russellville.

During his life, the impact Jungmeyer made on his community was recognized and appreciated by local residents. As the late L.A.B. Leslie, a fellow citizen of Russellville, wrote in a 1970s article, Arthur Jungmeyer deserved much of the credit for positive growth taking place in the town. "He has been active in every worthwhile project in the community, giving generously of his time and money," Leslie wrote. "If it has anything to do with Russellville, we know that we can count on Art."

TAMBKE PETROLEUM COMPANY

Served Russellville Area
for Several Decades

Situated on a hill when entering Russellville from the east along State Highway C is a building that has become a relic of the past. For many local residents, this now-closed service station represents a tireless individual who pursued several business interests while remaining dedicated to his family and community.

"My father, Herbert Tambke, was raised in Stover along with five siblings," said Fern Kirchner. "He later moved to Russellville and went to work as an agent for the Skelly Oil Company sometime before World War II, driving a truck to deliver bulk fuel to farmers."

Jim Tambke is pictured in front of the original Tambke Petroleum Company building opened by his father, Herbert, and his uncle, H.D., in 1950. Herbert was involved in many business interests in the Russellville area prior to his passing. *Fern Kirchner.*

Herbert later married Eunice Scrivner, and the couple purchased the home in Russellville in addition to farms south of town that had once belonged to a local dentist, Dr. George P. Tellman. When the war came to an end, Herbert's younger brother, H.D. Tambke, returned from his service with the Army Air Forces and joined his brother in a new business endeavor: the formation of the Tambke Petroleum Company. The company opened on July 15, 1950, in a building they had erected in the east end of Russellville. Fern Kirchner described how her father and mother, in addition to installing gas pumps and delivering various types of fuel, also operated a small diner that served sandwiches, coney dogs, hamburgers, chili and other such foods.

"Often, they would offer lunch plates," Fern Kirchner said. "There was also a counter with seats along with tables and chairs for the guests. On many weekends, all of the seats in the diner were taken up because we had one of the only televisions in town, and many local residents came to watch televised wrestling matches."

Fern's husband, Ray Kirchner, recalls being hired by Herbert to assist those visiting that station for fuel, with a focus on providing a full-service, quality experience for the customers. "When a customer pulled up, you

Herbert Tamkbe was forty-nine years old when he died in a tractor accident in 1959 while working on his farm south of Russellville. *Fern Kirchner.*

pumped their gas for them, checked their oil and washed their windshield," he said. "If you didn't do that, Herbert would make sure that you knew to do it next time." Smiling, he added, "When he said something, you listened."

Ray Kirchner said that Herbert Tambke was never one to rest on his laurels, soon expanding his business endeavors by hauling cattle to market in St. Louis for local farmers, then loading his truck with coal to bring back and sell upon his return.

"He built a stockyard behind the station where he could keep the cattle he was going to haul," Ray Kirchner said. "Other times, when I wasn't working at the station, I would go over to the farm and feed the livestock by filling the troughs."

Maintaining an interest in agriculture and serving local farmers, Tambke purchased a truck that had a mobile mill installed. He then established T&K Mobile Mill Service and traveled to local farms to mix feed for livestock. Fern Kirchner noted that in later years her father developed a small-scale salvage yard behind the shop, having spare vehicles in case parts were needed for repairs. Additionally, he built a building next to the station from which he operated a feed store for several years.

"It wasn't just business he was interested in," said Fern Kirchner. "He was always active in the community and served many years as the mayor of Russellville, helped establish the local Lion's Club and was a founding member of the volunteer fire department. He also hosted barbecues for the local high school baseball team and was active with Trinity Lutheran Church. My father was even an auctioneer, which was what his son Jim later decided to do."

Ray Kircher mirthfully added, "He was a good auctioneer because he talked so loud that everybody had to listen to him."

Adding to his array of talents and varied business interests, Tambke also served as an announcer at horse shows throughout the area. His daughter, who was learning to play the organ, was provided an opportunity to refine and display her musicianship at many of these events.

"My dad bought me an organ and I would go with him and play at horse shows around the circuit," she said. "Those are such good memories for me."

On September 10, 1959, Tambke was packing sileage in a silo on his farm south of Russellville. He was killed when the tractor he was using overturned. The forty-nine-year-old revered local citizen was laid to rest in nearby Enloe Cemetery. In his passing, he not only left behind his wife but also four children, the youngest of whom was only two years old. H.D., Tambke's younger brother, and his wife, Jacqueline, purchased Tambke Petroleum Company from Herbert's wife, Eunice, in August 1961. Under their ownership, the business underwent many additions, including a garage, service island and tire shop.

In the years following H.D.'s death, his son, David, ran the company. Although the business has been closed for a number of years, it remains an empty museum of sorts upon a hill entering Russellville, representing the last testament to Herbert Tambke and his involvement in the local community.

"My father was able to accomplish so much by the time he was forty-nine years old," said Fern Kirchner. "I was only sixteen years old when he passed, but I have so many great memories of him from childhood." She added, "His death shocked the entire community, and one thing I clearly recall is that so many people came to his funeral that they were standing outside of the church. I loved that man; he was so good to us."

Chapter 4

Religion

Cole Spring Baptist Church

Has Tended to Spiritual Needs of Russellville Area Since 1835

In 1831, the pioneering families of Enoch Enloe Sr. and Lamon decided to settle near the area that eventually became Russellville after a wheel on one of their covered wagons broke. Four years later, several families gathered on a nearby farm to establish the first church in the community. The Baptist congregation later moved to an area known as Belleville and helped establish several churches in the area. A handwritten church record notes that on June 27, 1835, local settlers met to formalize the formation of a congregation that would initially be known as Cold Spring Baptist Church, receiving its name from a spring in the area.

The record states, "Agreeable to a previous appointment, a number met at Brother [Jacob] Sawders' for the purpose of entering into a church covenant. As we believe that the scriptures plainly hold to view that prosperity of God's people living together in a church covenant, by giving ourselves to each other and the Lord."

It was at this meeting that fifteen "Articles of Faith" and twelve "Rules of Decorum" were adopted for the fledgling church and signed by John A. Langdon, Levi Roark, James Marcy, William Small and Louis Shelton.

In a *Russellville News* article from November 2, 1978, Bruce Murphy wrote, "The first church was erected on a farm now owned by Mr. George Rhodes.

The building faced the south and had two doors on the south, one for the men and one for the women." The original church building had one door on each end where African Americans, during a time associated with slavery and segregation, entered the building and worshiped alongside others from the community.

Three years after the church's founding, in 1838, the nearby town of Russellville came into existence after it was surveyed by land promoter and storekeeper Buckner Russell. The period of the Civil War was unnerving for many living in the vicinity of the church, since many joined companies of the Enrolled Missouri Militia in support of the Union, while guerrilla fighters loosely aligned with the Confederacy remained a constant threat. The effect of the war on the condition of the congregation is uncertain because there are no church records from this period.

"So much information we have is from family records of the descendants of the charter members," a written note in one of the church's history books reveals.

Oral histories handed down through the generations state the records from 1835 to 1883 perished in a fire, with no further details available. However, many businesses in nearby downtown Russellville burned to the ground in a major fire in 1883, and it is believed the records may have been held there, in one of the businesses owned by a church member.

The church became inspirational in the establishment of other church bodies, with Pleasant Hill being organized by Cold Spring Church in 1881. Several years later, in 1888, Mt. Olive Baptist Church, south of Russellville, was established through the assistance of members of Cold Springs.

"In 1889, the present site was chosen and a new building began," church records reveal. "Part of the old building was used in the construction of the [new] building. The building was completed in May 1890 and was dedicated September 28, 1890."

The site for the new church building was located within the fading community of Belleville on property donated by Andrew Jackson Leslie. The name of the church was eventually changed to Cole Springs Baptist Church, inspired by its location within Cole County. As a gift for Cole Springs' new location, First Baptist Church in Jefferson City donated their pulpit to the congregation. Belleville, which was established around 1880 with hopes the railroad would build a depot there, was located along State Highway V and once boasted a blacksmith shop, general store and houses. The town failed to grow when the railroad depot was instead established in nearby Russellville.

Cole Spring Baptist Church has a legacy dating back to 1835. It has not only ministered to several generations but also helped establish four other Baptist churches in the area. *Jeremy Amick.*

The rural church made headlines in the *St. Louis Post-Dispatch* on October 5, 1897. "Two young men nearly twenty-one years old…are locked in jail under the fines of $25 and costs each for being drunk and disturbing religious worship at Cole Spring Baptist Church near Russellville….The preacher had them arrested and they pleaded guilty in Justice court. Their parents refused to pay their fines because they thought the boys needed punishing."

Throughout the next several years, services continued without major distraction, and the congregation helped establish Russellville Baptist Church in 1903, followed by Corticelli Baptist Church in 1905.

There is a pause in church records from the period of early October 1918 to April 1919, revealing a suspension in monthly business meetings and worship services. It was during this period in U.S. history that not only did World War I come to an end, but the spread of the Spanish Flu caused worldwide closures of houses of worship.

On August 29, 1937, Cole Spring held their centennial celebration (two years late), which had an attendance estimated at more than five hundred people. The principal speaker at the celebration was Congressman William Lester Nelson, a native of Bunceton, Missouri.

John B. Rollins is pictured with his wife, Doris, during the sesquicentennial celebration at Cole Spring Baptist Church in 1985. Rollins pastored several Baptist churches during his career, including Cole Spring. *Cole Spring Baptist Church.*

Theological author Eddie Gibbs wrote, "Old churches must not simply stand as monuments to the past but as spiritual grandparents that have invested in the future by passing on their life to others and releasing their offspring to form new congregations."

Cole Spring Baptist Church, though a small congregation, has a spiritual influence that has weighed mightily throughout the decades by helping establish other congregations. Her doors, though creaking with a little age, remain open to the community and continue to welcome all to worship, just as she has for nearly two centuries.

St. Paul's Lutheran Church in Lohman

Founded by German Immigrants in 1852

During the 1840s, scores of hopeful individuals departed their German homeland in pursuit of the promise of a better life in the United States. Many eventually settled in the community that in later years became known as Lohman, bringing with them their Lutheran faith and establishing a church "on the hill" that has weathered the decades and continues to serve a dedicated congregation.

"It was in the year 1852, that the desire to perpetuate the Lutheran faith brought together the heads of a number of emigrant families in the Stringtown area of west-central Cole County, Missouri," noted the *History of St. Paul's Church*, printed in 1977. "Residents of the area since the previous decade, these Bavarians, Westphalians, Saxons and Austrians, dreamed of the establishment of a real church, one in which the catechism could be taught, marriages and burials celebrated in a traditional manner, and in which their firmly held belief in Grace and Justification would find expression."

These families found assistance through Rev. J.P. Kalb, who was at the time serving as pastor of Zion Lutheran Church near Jefferson City, in addition to providing spiritual guidance to several congregations in the outlying rural areas.

The new St. Paul's Evangelical Lutheran Church, part of the Missouri Synod, was organized following a meeting of several families in the home of the Plochberger family. Reverend Carl W.R. Frederking was installed as pastor on April 28, 1852, serving in that capacity for the next three years.

Hardscrabble parishioners worked to erect the first church on the western slope of a hill overlooking the area that years later became Lohman. The first church structure, history notes, was of simple log construction, and it provided a spiritual home to the congregation for nearly two decades. The latter part of the Civil War proved to be a trying period for the growing church since two of their members—Friedrich Strobel and Erhardt Kautsch—died of wounds received from Confederate troops under the command of General Sterling Price near Stringtown on October 8, 1864. Both were buried in the church cemetery.

"It was during these closing days of the Civil War that doctrinal disputes caused the separation of St. Paul's Church from membership in the Missouri Synod, and saw it join the Synod of Iowa," said the 1977 church history booklet.

Several of the original members chose to break away from St. Paul's and, in 1867, organized St. John's Lutheran Church in nearby Stringtown, the latter congregation maintaining an association with the Missouri Synod.

In 1871, construction began on a new church building for St. Paul's, a stone structure erected from materials quarried by members of the congregation. An important milestone in the church's history came in late summer 1875 with the arrival of Reverend George Fikenscher, who still holds the distinction as the longest-serving pastor for the church.

Members of the congregation watched as a village grew up near the town with the advent of the railroad spur. The community soon earned the designation of Lohman in the early 1880s because of the post office established by businessman Charles W. Lohman.

During the nearly thirty years Reverend Fikenscher served St. Paul's, a schoolhouse was built, along with a second parsonage. The school would later close, with students receiving their education either at nearby Lohman

Members of St. Paul's erected a schoolhouse in 1880 under the ministry of Reverend George Fikenscher. Pictured is one of the classes from around the year 1900. *Gert Strobel.*

School or by traveling to Jefferson City or Russellville. Retiring from the ministry on December 31, 1904, Reverend Fikenscher spent his remaining years in the Lohman area. The German native was eighty-two years old when he died in 1922, and he is interred in the cemetery of St. Paul's Lutheran Church. The year following Fikenscher's death, the decision was made to erect a new church.

"Gus Linsenbardt, who served as foreman for the construction of the church, says that the stone steeple from the original church was retained when the new church was built and that the steeple was covered with a brick veneer so that it would match the newly constructed brick church," reported the *Daily Capital News* on July 30, 1977. "Within nine months, the church was completed and was officially dedicated on November 16, 1924."

Gus Fischer, a longtime member of the congregation at St. Paul's, was confirmed on April 9, 1952, and witnessed the transition from some of the traditional services at the church. Records indicate that worship services were conducted entirely in German until the late 1920s.

"When I was real young, I can remember that there was a German service about once a month, but sometime around the late 1940s, that stopped entirely and they were done in English only," Fischer said. "Also, I remember we used to take communion about once a quarter, but now that is done every Sunday."

St. Paul's Lutheran Church grew exponentially after its founding in 1852. The congregation currently uses their third house of worship, a brick building that was dedicated in 1924. *Gert Strobel.*

The same church building that has served the congregation since 1924 continues to provide a home for their fellowship and Sunday classes, although the building has undergone renovations and additions throughout the years.

The late Gertrude Strobel, who was ninety-six years old when she passed away in 2020, served in many capacities within the church but was best known for being the organist since 1946. An ardent devotee to her Lutheran faith, she composed words of praise for the church's one hundredth anniversary celebration in 1952, awestruck by the longevity of the congregation established by her German forebearers.

Ope' wide the door, Ope' wide the door,
For there is no stranger here,
Worship with us and let it e'er be,
(Closer) to his temple draw near.

Loudly we sing, Loudly we sing,
As the organ rolls forth loud and strong,
With ever joyful hearts we thank our God,
So join in the everlasting song.

St. John's Lutheran Church

Stringtown Congregation Rises from the Ashes of Dissension in 1867

During the Civil War, dissension began to foment within the congregation of St. Paul's Lutheran Church in Lohman. St. Paul's was organized in 1852 by German immigrants. Doctrinal disputes resulted in the decision of some congregants to leave the Missouri Synod and join the Iowa Synod. Choosing to maintain an association with the Missouri Synod, several of the founding members of St. Paul's split away from the church and later organized St. John's Lutheran Church in nearby Stringtown on July 24, 1867.

"For the founders of St. John's…this was the second organizing procedure in which they had taken part in a fifteen-year period," according to a booklet printed in celebration of the St. John's sesquicentennial in 2017. "Since the members who withdrew their memberships from their former congregation were on their own and desiring to remain in the Lutheran Church-Missouri Synod, they accepted the services of Pastor [Emil] Wege, who was pastor of Zion Lutheran Church, Jefferson City."

A church constitution was written and approved, while a frame church was constructed to provide a worship site for the fledgling congregation. As the church continued to grow, several pastors answered the call to serve at St. John's and conducted baptisms, confirmations and burials in addition to holding services in the German language. Tragedy occurred fifteen years after the church's founding, while Pastor John August Proft was serving as pastor for the congregation. His wife, Dorothea Margaretha Henrietta, died during childbirth on April 17, 1882, when she was only thirty years old. She was laid to rest with her unborn child in the church cemetery under a beautiful monument featuring an angel pointing to the heavens while comforting a small girl.

The first church building lasted only eight years; it was struck by lightning in 1872 and burned to the ground. The second church, another wood-frame structure, was erected in 1872 and served the congregation until 1905.

"In 1902, it was concluded that the frame Church had become inadequate, for it needed many major and costly repairs and was difficult to heat," noted a church pamphlet printed in 1955. "So, the decision was made to begin planning for its replacement."

A building fund was established, and the decision was made to replace the frame structure with a new church made from brick and stone. John

The third church of St. John's Lutheran Church is pictured under construction in 1905. Standing next to the ladder (*at left*) is John Scheperle Sr. of Millbrook, who served as architect and builder. *Susan Scheperle Schenewerk.*

J. Scheperle Sr., a member of the congregation who had helped erect Centennial Mill in nearby Millbrook, was chosen to serve as the architect and builder of the new church. Stone for the foundation was quarried on property owned by the church, a large part of the lumber was donated and the bricks were purchased. Construction began in the spring of 1905. Later that year, on December 10, dedication services were held with Scheperle presenting the key to the church door to Pastor John H. Mueller.

This church building continues to serve the congregation of St. John's Lutheran Church, although there have been additions and remodeling to the original structure throughout the last several decades.

"When I was younger, I can remember that we had about one church service in German every month," said Edgar Kautsch, a member of the 1949 confirmation class for St. John's. His father, Gustav Kautsch, was confirmed at the church in 1914. Reflecting on the many changes he's witnessed in the last several decades, Kautsch added, "The men used to sit on the right side of the church and the women on the left. There also used to be communion about once a month, then it went to every other Sunday and now it's done every Sunday."

A parsonage was erected in 1898 to provide a home for the pastors and their families. This was replaced in 1913 with a second parsonage, built by John Scheperle Jr., the son of the builder of the current church building.

This parsonage has undergone several updates but is still utilized for its original purpose. Providing a parochial education to the students of the congregation also became a focus early in the church's history. The first schoolhouse was a whitewashed wooden building erected in 1894. In 1915, it was replaced by a brick schoolhouse that taught "the four *R*'s"—reading, (w)riting, (a)rithmetic and religion.

"I attended my first three years of classes at Stringtown School before starting classes at the St. John's schoolhouse," Kautsch recalled. "I attended the church school for four years until Pastor [Clifford] Bliss left in the late 1940s. Then I completed the eighth grade at Lohman and then went to Russellville High School."

The school at St. John's closed in 1952 following consolidation of local school districts. The building was torn down by a contractor in 1990. A small canopy has since been dedicated at the site of the former schoolhouse, which houses the bell once used to signal students to classes.

The church building has been expanded and a new parish hall constructed. In 1985, Pastor Warren Brandt, a Wisconsin native and U.S. Air Force veteran, answered the call to serve at St. John's. He remained with the congregation for twenty-eight years and is, thus far, the longest serving of any pastor in church history.

Built in 1915, this was the second of two schoolhouses used to provide an education to students in the congregation. This building was torn down in 1990. *St. John's Lutheran Church.*

Generations of local residents continue to pass through the doors of St. John's Lutheran Church for worship and fellowship. It is a heritage, as noted in the one hundredth anniversary booklet printed in 1967, highlighted by an impressive legacy of service and faith: "O, what beauty, therefore, is found in each and every footstep which we would trace as we open our 'History Book of God's Love,' and, by His Spirit, see how He would write each 'Year of His Grace' indelibly upon our souls…"

RUSSELLVILLE UNITED METHODIST CHURCH

Began Legacy of Spiritual Service in 1836

The history of the Methodist denomination in the Russellville area dates back to the pioneer days in Missouri, when a congregation was organized in 1836, through the efforts of circuit pastors. Initially lacking their own house of worship, these early Methodists shared a log cabin a short distance west of town with Cold Spring Baptist Church (later renamed "Cole" Spring), another small congregation that formed a year earlier.

"By 1839, the group had grown sufficiently to warrant the appointment of a local pastor to shepherd the young congregation," noted Russellville's sesquicentennial book. "Records show that the Reverend Albert [Wilson] Rhoads, great-grandfather of Freeman Kraus, was selected for the position; he moved with his family from Tennessee to Russellville in 1839 and assumed leadership of the parish."

The twenty-five-year-old Rhoads settled on a farm south of Russellville, near the spring that inspired the name of Cold Spring Baptist Church. During Rhoads's tenure as pastor, the fledgling Methodist congregation faced an important milestone in 1844 and split over the issue of slavery.

"In 1844 when the Methodist Episcopal Church separated into the MEC and the MEC South, Missouri officially went South," explained the Missouri United Methodist Archives. "Both churches operated in Missouri, many times side-by-side in the same town until 1939 when they were reunited."

Any early divisions among the Methodists did not prevent the growth of the church on the local level, where the congregation acquired two lots in Russellville in March 1851 and erected their first church building.

According to a church historical booklet, "The warranty deed provided… said [the] property was to be used as both a Methodist Church and community school."

On January 1, 1855, forty-year-old Reverend Rhoads passed away unexpectedly after providing more than fifteen years of spiritual leadership. He was laid to rest on his farm south of Russellville, where his wife and some of his grandchildren were later interred. Their graves were eventually moved to Enloe Cemetery, west of Russellville.

Not only did the United Methodist Church serve as the first church within Russellville proper, but led by James Banister, an area merchant, the Methodist congregation also established the first Sunday school in the community in 1858. Thirty-seven years later, another denomination would build their own church in the town.

The Miller County Autogram-Sentinel noted on August 6, 1885, "The Cumberland Presbyterian Church at Russellville…will be dedicated by Rev. R.B. Ward [on August 9, 1885]." The establishment of this church, located on the corner of Simpson and McDavitt Streets, later provided an opportunity for the local Methodists.

The small white frame church the Methodist congregation built in Russellville was located on a tract of land southeast of the intersection of Jefferson and Smith Streets. The building served the faithful flock until the early 1920s and, during its more than seventy years of use, not only provided a worship site but was also used to hold classes for the local school district.

"Harold K. Carnish, the evangelist who has been holding a revival meeting at the Russellville Methodist Church, closed the meeting Sunday evening with thirteen additions to the church," noted the *Daily Capital News* on November 17, 1920. "Evangelist Carnish was a good entertainer, as well as a good preacher, and his meetings were attended nightly by large audiences."

The original church building had outgrown its small size and was disassembled, with much of the material used in the construction of a nearby home. The Methodist congregation then acquired the building a few blocks to the southwest that had been used by the Cumberland Presbyterian Church, whose congregation had disbanded.

Fern Kirchner, a longtime member of the Russellville United Methodist Church, shared, "One of the most emotional moments I remember is the funeral of Johnny Campbell, a local man whose family was part of our congregation." A 1964 graduate of Russellville High School, John Allen Campbell was killed on August 13, 1967, while serving with the United States Marine Corps in Vietnam. His body was returned to Russellville and interred in nearby Enloe Cemetery.

Another notable historical moment came in October 1984 with the beginning of an auspicious expansion and improvement project for

Established in 1836 by circuit pastors, the Russellville United Methodist Church continues to serve the spiritual needs of area residents. In 1986, the church began a major two-year restoration project. *Fern Kirchner.*

the church. As noted in Russellville's sesquicentennial book, "The current facilities were expanded and completely restored from the footings and foundation to the cross on top of the steeple."

The overall project took two years to complete at a cost of more than $75,000, and it was consecrated during a Sunday service held on June 1, 1986.

The same year the restoration was finished, the members of the church honored the man who ushered their predecessors through the congregation's formative years. A large cedar cross was erected at the burial site of their first pastor, Albert Rhoads, on the farm south of town where he lived until his death in 1855. The cross included the inscription: "Rev. Albert Rhoads, 1814–1855, a Methodist Minister Lies Here."

Since she was just a young girl, Fern Kirchner has been actively involved with the church and has fulfilled such roles as historian and organist. She recognizes that the congregation's Methodist forebearers played an important role in both the spiritual and physical growth of the community and hopes that it is a legacy honored by future generations.

"Someday, there will be young people who are going to want to know more about the past," she said. "If it's not in writing, a lot of the older people will be gone and there will be no one for them to ask their questions." She concluded, "That's why it is important for us to help make sure the history of our church is preserved for them."

RUSSELLVILLE BAPTIST CHURCH

Founded through Help of Nearby Congregation

On the evening of April 9, 1903, a group from the Russellville area gathered at the Presbyterian Church (now the Russellville United Methodist Church). Many came from nearby Cole Spring Baptist Church and were interested in organizing a new Baptist church in Russellville. The vision discussed in this meeting soon became a reality, serving as the defining moment for a new congregation that has since provided for the spiritual needs of several generations of congregants.

"The organizational worship service was held on May 10, 1903, at the Presbyterian Church," wrote Mark Weber in a pamphlet titled *Brief Highlights of the First 100 Years of Russellville Baptist Church: 1903–2003*. He added, "In August 1903, the church voted to request membership in the Concord Baptist Association, and messengers were selected to attend that body."

Within a couple years of its founding, the congregation raised the $350 necessary to purchase property on the corner of Simpson and Grace Streets. By the fall of 1906, a new church building had been completed on the property at the total cost of $1,499.35. Sadly, tragedy struck in 1906 when twenty-year-old Semerida E. Leslie unexpectedly passed away and was buried in the Russellville City Cemetery. Her father, Dr. Joseph Samuel Leslie, a local physician and member of the fledgling congregation, donated a bell to the church in memory of his daughter. The bell was installed in the belfry of the original church building.

Russellville Baptist Church was formed in 1906 through the assistance of members of nearby Cole Spring Baptist Church. Pictured is the original church building, demolished in 2000. *Jim and Eve Campbell.*

"A Sunday School was organized on February 29, 1908," said Russellville's sesquicentennial book. "Up until this time, members were attending a union Sunday School at the Presbyterian Church."

Growth remained a welcome and consistent theme in the early years of the church. In 1912, when the church was only nine years old, it had a recorded membership of 133. The following year, congregational records reveal that a revival was held and "there were 60 additions to the church."

In November 1918, the decision was made to postpone the meeting to determine whether to retain the current pastor. At the time, churches nationwide, though celebrating the recent end of World War I, were closing their doors as the Spanish influenza spread at an alarming rate. The church voted to align with the Southern Baptist Convention in 1919. The next several years were defined by additions to the congregational membership and repairs being made to the church building. However, the advent of the Great Depression heralded a brief period of financial uncertainty.

After being called to order and taking care of some general business, "our pastor then retired from the building that church might plan their business for the coming year," noted church minutes from November 18, 1933. "Brother Roscoe Campbell was elected as moderator and a vote was taken as to whether we should have preaching services twice a month or only once a month. There were 20 votes for twice a month and nine votes for once a month. Then a motion was made that we hire Brother Pierce for one-half time providing we could arrange to pay him."

Further financial difficulties followed. The church minutes of June 23, 1934, explain, "A motion was made and seconded to release Brother Pierce from our service as we didn't have enough money to pay him for his service here."

Monetary concerns carried forth throughout the next few years, but the church was able to weather the storm. The congregation later purchased property adjacent to their original plot and, in 1955, dedicated a parsonage. A new educational building was erected north of the church in 1962 and, the following year, a vote was taken to remove the outdoor toilet that had been used by the congregation in earlier years. During this period, a baptistry was also installed; thus, the church no longer required the use of local creeks to perform baptisms.

"I was about six years old when we started going to Russellville Baptist Church," said Mark Weber. "At that time, the old white church was the only building on the property, there wasn't any plumbing in the building and we still used the old outhouse behind the building."

More space was needed for the growing church body, and in 1983, a new addition with classrooms was added. The parsonage was demolished in 1987 to provide space for a new sanctuary.

"It wasn't an easy decision to tear down the old church," recalled Mark Weber. "There was a lot of sentimental attachment to the old building, but it got to the point of spending a lot of money for upkeep, and it just wasn't large enough for our sanctuary purposes."

The original sanctuary was demolished in 2000, and a new addition was built that housed office space and additional meeting areas. Doors and much of the wood trim from the original church were salvaged and used in the new addition. The church bell was saved and, although now in storage, will likely be placed on display in the coming years.

Like most churches in the area, Russellville Baptist Church has experienced its assorted hardships and victories, but during its lengthy history, one constant has been its continued growth and focus on sharing the Gospel.

"Our church has experienced its ups and downs throughout the years—like any church does," said Mark Weber. "During the Great Depression, the records show that there were some monetary issues and overall lean times." Pausing, he added, "But through it all, we have survived and continue to be actively involved in providing a positive influence in the local community."

Trinity Lutheran Church in Russellville

A Home to Devoted Congregation Since 1895

In 1895, John J. Buchta and Michael Schubert, both of German descent and actively engaged in business endeavors in the Russellville area, began the work of organizing a Lutheran church. Scores of German immigrants and their descendants had already established Lutheran churches in nearby communities such as Lohman and Stringtown. These trustees sought to form a new house of worship, one that would soon become a centerpiece of community involvement in Russellville.

"Pastor (Paul) Franke conducted services September 1, 1895, although the congregation was not yet fully organized," wrote Dr. Roger Jungmeyer, a professor of history at Lincoln University, in an application for inclusion of the church in the National Register of Historic Places. "During the same time Trinity at Russellville was being organized [Pastor Franke] was serving a church at California, Missouri."

A congregation began to assemble, with church records revealing that the first funeral and burial was conducted on October 28, 1895, followed by the first baptism on November 3, 1895. A one-acre plot of land was purchased on the west side of Marion Street in Russellville, where a small frame church and a parsonage were erected.

Based upon records maintained by Pastor Franke, the first church was dedicated on September 13, 1896, and was celebrated by two services: a morning worship service conducted in German and an afternoon service in English.

Schubert and Buchta, on behalf of the growing congregation, acquired two acres of land south of Russellville on September 12, 1896, and established the church cemetery. Frederick Schardt and Charles Schober would later serve the congregation as pastors, but it was under the guidance of Reverend C. Schaff, who received his call to Trinity in 1910, that the congregation's arc of growth continued unabated.

"In 1911, an opportunity presented itself to sell the old church property for $2,500.00," noted a "Historical Sketch" featured in the church's *Golden Jubilee* booklet from 1945. "On March 26, this offer was accepted. Steps were immediately taken to build first the parsonage on the new ground [its current location]…with eight rooms and a solid brick structure costing the congregation the sum of $1,900.00."

The parsonage was dedicated in early October 1911, and only a few days later, the cornerstone was laid for the new church building. The brick church, measuring thirty-six by seventy feet and featuring two spires, was dedicated on August 4, 1912. The church was situated just east of the parsonage, facing the unpaved "Old Versailles Road" (now State Highway C).

Later the same year, a white one-room schoolhouse was dedicated, and it was used for confirmation classes for a number of years; however, it has more recently been utilized as an office, as a meeting space and for storage. Years later, on July 4, 1923, another important moment in the early history of the church began.

It was on this date that Reverend F. Otto Rossbach "from Stuttgart, Kansas, assumed the ministry of the congregation," according to the church's seventy-fifth anniversary booklet from 1970. "Two important personal events during the time of his pastorate were his marriage to Miss Hattie Schlutz on October 29, 1924, and the ordination of his son Walter (a child from a previous marriage) in 1938."

Reverend Rossbach earned the distinction of being the longest-serving pastor for Trinity Lutheran Church in Russellville, remaining with the

Above: The second—and current—church for Trinity Lutheran Church in Russellville was dedicated in 1912, nearly seventeen years after the church was established. The church and parsonage are pictured on the day of dedication. *Trinity Lutheran Church.*

Left: From 1923 to 1944, Reverend F. Otto Rossbach served as pastor for Trinity Lutheran Church and holds the distinction of being the longest-serving pastor in church history. *Trinity Lutheran Church.*

congregation from 1923 to 1944. During World War II, his son, Walter, volunteered as a chaplain in the Canadian Army.

The seventy-eight-year-old Reverend Rossbach passed away in 1948 and was laid to rest in Saint Peter Cemetery in New Richland, Minnesota. On May 11, 1940, during Rossbach's tenure at Trinity, the parish hall was dedicated on land donated by the widow of Michael Schubert, whose husband helped organize the church decades earlier.

Reverend John J. Haberaecker accepted a call to serve the congregation in 1945. Church records reveal a number of changes made during his ministry, which included the complete transition to English-language worship services, while the long-embraced German-language services were reserved for special occasions.

"At a congregational meeting in July 1955, plans were approved for a rock veneer building in the cemetery to be used for storage and shelter; a rock entrance to the cemetery and shrubbery had been added earlier," said the seventy-fifth anniversary booklet.

Due to illness, Haberaecker's sixteen-year ministry ended in 1961, and the next two decades witnessed the spiritual leadership of Reverends Robert G. Wessels, Harold Martens and Howard Ellis. During the seventy-fifth anniversary worship on August 16, 1970, Reverend Walter Rossbach, whose father had served as pastor more than a quarter century earlier, conducted a special service honoring the church's longevity.

The last few decades have witnessed many improvements made to the church and parish hall, restoration of the schoolhouse and the construction of a garage and pavilion. In 2020, the church celebrated its 125th anniversary and, through the research and dedication of Dr. Roger Jungmeyer, has earned designation as a historic district in the National Register of Historic Places. The church turned to the late Erna Raithel, a longtime congregation member and pillar of the community, for the words which best describe the blessings that Trinity Lutheran Church has both given and received during its years of ministry: "May Trinity in the coming years continue to be a blessing to its members and to the community of which it is a part; may Trinity continue to be loyal and devoted to carrying out the commands of its loving Savior; and may Trinity always express praise and Thanksgiving to our faithful God."

ST. MICHAEL'S CATHOLIC CHURCH

Established through Help of Missionary Priest

The legacy of St. Michael's Catholic Church in Russellville began in earnest during the 1860s, with the founding of the Catholic mission of St. Joseph's on the eastern edge of Stringtown. A small group of immigrant families met in a log church on a hill west of the North Moreau River, where mass was held every few weeks. The final mass was conducted at the Stringtown church in 1894 as new Catholic parishes were established in nearby communities.

Father John Schramm, a German immigrant and assistant pastor of St. Peter's Parish in Jefferson City, was one of the missionary priests who traveled to Stringtown to lead mass. He was not only instrumental in establishing the parish in St. Martin's in 1885 but also helped guide Russellville area Catholics in the formation of their own parish in 1887.

"On October 15, 1887, $100 was donated by five individuals and paid to [Basil] McDavitt and Elizabeth McDavitt for a parcel of land deeded to trustees of the Catholic Church…in the town of Russellville, for the purpose of establishing a Catholic community," according to Russellville's sesquicentennial book. "The deed was filed for record on October 26, 1887; and the same year a stone was laid by Reverend Schramm, symbolizing the intent to build a church and Catholic parish there."

The congregation of St. Michael's in Russellville used contributions and money raised through picnics to cover the costs of constructing a wood-frame church on a one-and-a-half-acre lot, which was dedicated on October 22, 1890. They were also able to purchase an additional parcel of property in 1891, moving a small schoolhouse from Stringtown to the site.

"In 1906, St. Michael's was established as a parish," stated a church directory printed in 1987. "Up until then, it had been a mission of St. Martin's."

Father John Wehner, the first pastor for St. Michael's, began his ministry in Russellville

Father John Schramm laid a symbolic cornerstone for the first church built for the St. Michael's Catholic mission in Russellville in 1887. *Jim and Eve Campbell.*

in 1901, the same year he was ordained. The priest remained with the congregation until they became a parish in 1906. Sadly, he passed away in 1933, when he was only fifty-six years of age. Continuing to grow, the parish was blessed with the resources to construct a rectory while also having a resident priest to perform many administrative functions and conduct masses. However, as noted in the August 30, 1934 edition of the *Central Missourian*, services were discontinued at St. Michael's following the departure of Father Reh in September 1933.

"Regular services are to again be resumed at St. Michael's Catholic Church…beginning next Sunday, July 8 at 10 a.m.," reported the *Central Missourian* on July 5, 1934. "Father Edward A. Bruemmer, assistant pastor at St. Peter's Church in Jefferson City, will take charge of the spiritual and financial matters of the parish."

Under the leadership of Father Bruemmer, the parish remained vibrant. Throughout the next several years, a number of competent administrators, most coming from nearby St. Peter's Catholic Church, were assigned to the Russellville congregation for mass and other religious services in addition to conducting confirmation classes.

Father Schramm, a Catholic priest and German immigrant, helped establish the mission in Russellville that became St. Michael's Catholic Church. *Jim and Eve Campbell.*

Reverend Norman Ahrens, administrator of St. Michael's, wrote to the congregation on May 9, 1968, "The building of the parish hall is now taking place in earnest. Needless to say, the new hall will be most welcomed."

Two years later, the once bustling parish, having only recently completed the new parish hall, was closed. In a letter to parishioners dated February 13, 1970, Reverend Michael McAuliffe described the circumstances leading to the difficult decision. "When I came into the Diocese, I found that we were faced with an immediate shortage of priests, and as you know, this effects the Church everywhere," Reverend McAuliffe wrote. "In light of these facts and with the growing demand that smaller parishes be amalgamated into larger ones for the benefit of both priest and people…I must close this parish and assign you, its parishioners, to St. Martins Parish."

The parish at St. Michael's remained closed for nearly fifteen years, reopening on December 24, 1984, under the leadership of Father Mel Lahr. The parish has since remained an integral component of the local community, experiencing steady levels of growth in recent years. The old schoolhouse, church and rectory have long since been demolished, but the property has undergone many updates and improvements that include a new church and parish house.

The passage of time has brought much change, but the St. Michael's parish maintains a connection to its early roots. The church continues to care for the small cemetery on a hill overlooking the North Moreau in Stringtown, where many early Catholic immigrants were buried adjacent to a bygone log church.

"It's a wonderful history and a parish that I am proud to have been a member of since 1985," said Sharon Murphy. "It's always been so easy to make friends here and work with others—everyone just jumps right in to help when there is a project to be done."

The church's mission statement aptly describes its role in the tapestry of Russellville's history, along with its dedication to the community: "We are committed to the spiritual growth of all parishioners and are called to be messengers to others of God's peace, love, and forgiveness in our lives. We welcome opportunities to cooperate with other faith communities."

CHAPTER 5

POTLUCK OF HISTORY

BAVARIAN IMMIGRANTS MURDERED NEAR LOHMAN DURING THE LATTER PART OF THE CIVIL WAR

William Tecumseh Sherman, a renowned Union general who served during the Civil War, has been credited with the simple, unadorned quote: "War is hell." An apt description of the atrocities faced by soldiers serving on both sides of the bloody conflict, Sherman's quote encapsulates the destruction that the "War Between the States" levied upon the countryside and which occasionally led to deadly consequences even for those not wearing a military uniform.

Two Bavarian immigrants living in Lohman during the Civil War are an example of how the blood of innocents was spilled throughout the Missouri landscape, often leaving behind grieving widows and children.

"Friedrich Strobel and Ehrhardt Kautsch were born near the small city of Naila in northeastern Bavaria (now Germany)," said Don Buchta of Lohman, a retired schoolteacher and local historian.

According to Buchta's research, Strobel, born in 1825, married Anna Emilie Kautsch—the sister of Ehrhardt Kautsch—while still living in Bavaria. Said Buchta, "Kautsch then became the brother-in-law to Strobel through marriage."

Kautsch, born in 1815, married Elizabeth Thor, and both couples went on to raise several children, some of whom were born in Bavaria, others in the United States. In 1857, Strobel and Kautsch escaped the social and political unrest plaguing their homeland by joining the mass migration to the United

States, settling in what became the German Lutheran community of Lohman. The two families resided together in a log cabin, a portion of which, Buchta said, still exists.

Little evidence documents the lives of the two men prior to the onset of the Civil War, but Buchta's research helps shed some light on a deadly encounter involving soldiers associated with a Confederate general. Based upon interviews with descendants (now deceased) and church records, Buchta ascertained that on October 8, 1864, Strobel and Kautsch saddled their horses and embarked for the nearby community of Stringtown—a bustling community at that time—to pick up supplies. That is when they encountered several troops under the command of General Sterling Price.

Friedrich Strobel (pictured) and his brother-in-law, Ehrhardt Kautsch, emigrated from Bavaria to Lohman in 1857. They were later killed during an encounter with General Sterling Price's forces outside of Lohman. *Don and Roger Buchta.*

According to information gleaned from the Missouri State Historical Society's website, General Price, who had previously served as governor of Missouri, was leading an expedition into Missouri with the intent of capturing Union-controlled territories for the Confederacy, including the state capitol. As Kautsch and Strobel approached Price's troop near the outskirts of Stringtown, "they were given the order to halt, but did not obey the command," Buchta said. "Price's troops opened fire. They then took [Strobel's and Kautsch's] horses and rode away."

Struck in the chest by a bullet, Kautsch is believed to have died immediately. Strobel received a bullet wound to his head and was taken to the nearby home of Johann Pistel—who had also emigrated from Germany—where he passed away the following day. An article printed in the *Missouri State Times* on October 15, 1864, stated Price's troops were "occasionally guilty of cold-blooded murders" and mentions the deaths of both Strobel and Kautsch (though misspelling their names), describing the two as "Germans who resided in the vicinity of Gordon and Eans mill."

History shows that Price's expedition through Missouri in the latter part of 1864 resulted in several major defeats and extensive casualties among his forces, but the impact of the actions of those under his command reverberated throughout the Lohman community.

"Kautsch left behind a wife and four daughters and Strobel a wife and five children," said Gert Strobel, a historian for St. Paul's Lutheran Church, while reviewing a church listing of obituaries covering the period of 1852–1983.

History books are peppered with accounts of the significant number of deaths that occurred because of the Civil War—a conflict that took the lives of roughly 2 percent of the nation's population, an estimated 620,000 individuals. But often lost in such statistics is the cost that many local communities were forced to bear when innocent civilians were robbed of their futures, leaving behind families and neighbors to cope with the unexpected losses.

The deaths of Strobel and Kautsch serve as a depressing tale of two Bavarian immigrants departing the hardships of their native country in search of a better life in America. Though cut down in their prime more than 150 years ago, this story of the cold-blooded murder of two innocent men remains, to this day, a frequent topic of discussion and intrigue throughout the rural, German-influenced community of Lohman.

TRAIN WRECKS

1881 and 1937 Train Accidents Mark Dark Moments in Russellville Railroad History

The years after the Civil War were an exciting time in the history of Russellville, since the Missouri Pacific Railroad provided a means for the community to receive and ship assorted commodities. In 1879, the construction of the Bagnell Branch began, which was intended to stretch from Jefferson City to Lebanon. Despite the economic prosperity resulting from this new transportation network, the railroad, on two separate occasions, became the antagonist in the story of the town.

"The track was completed to Russellville by July 1881," noted the late Arthur Jungmeyer in Russellville's sesquicentennial book. "After reaching the Osage River at Bagnell, it was decided to go no farther."

The depot building in Russellville became a focal point of community activity. With the availability of stock shipping and eventually, passenger service, a booming downtown grew up along the tracks. Many of these brick buildings that once housed businesses such as a hotel, mercantile and banks are still part of the historical downtown area. Early in its history, prior to

A tragic railroad accident along the Bagnell Branch of the Missouri Pacific Railroad occurred in 1881 east of Russellville, killing four individuals. Among them was Green Berry, a Jefferson City farmer and former county sheriff. *Jim and Eve Campbell.*

attaining the name "Bagnell Branch," the stretch of railroad was referred to as the "Jefferson City, Lebanon and Southwestern Railroad." Shortly after completion of the rail line through Russellville, the first moment of tragedy unfolded on December 18, 1881.

"A Ride to Death" proclaimed the headline of an article in the December 19, 1881 edition of the *St. Louis Globe-Democrat.* The article explained that the citizens of Jefferson City had been "thrown into a fever of intense and anxious excitement by the news of the most appalling calamity that has visited this section in many years."

A train, consisting of the engine, tender, six flat cars, a boxcar and a coach, was headed to the then-terminus of the track near Russellville to deliver a load of railroad iron. Along for the trip were four citizens of Jefferson City: Green C. Berry, Chris Wagner, Oscar Monnig and Willie Zuendt. They made a brief stop in Lohman to pick up railroad employee Chris Gemeinhardt. Upon reaching Russellville, the iron was unloaded, and the locomotive began to push the cars back toward Jefferson City (since the tracks terminated and there was no way to turn around). The return trip started out rather uneventful but quickly devolved into a catastrophe.

"About two miles east of Russellville, at 12:14 p.m., the engine and tender jumped the track, ran along the track for about 100 feet, tearing up the rails," wrote Arthur Jungmeyer. "The tender and the cab of the engine fell off the embankment; the engine, totally wrecked, came to rest across the tracks."

The passengers had been sitting upon makeshift seats on the front flat car. When the wreck occurred, the flat car was pushed across the engine and immediately killed Wagner, Berry and Monnig. The reports reveal their dreadful death, mangled and scalded by the steam of the engine. Gemeinhardt and Zuendt were taken to a nearby home for emergency treatment; Gemeinhardt passed away a short time later. The day following the accident, the *St. Louis Globe* noted, "Conductor Vaughan was in the box car with others at the time, but, though it turned completely over, none of its occupants were injured beyond a few bruises."

The accident sent ripples through the Jefferson City community since Green C. Berry (namesake of Green Berry Road) was a respected farmer who had served as the county sheriff and collector. Wagner had served his county as treasurer and was a prominent grocer in Jefferson City.

More than fifty years passed without a major rail incident in the area while passenger and freight service continued to support the needs of the community. In the late 1920s, the tracks were busy hauling supplies for the construction of the Bagnell Dam. However, during the latter part of the Great Depression, another accident, this one with a less critical outcome, unfolded near Russellville. Describing the accident that occurred on March 22, 1937, the *Jefferson City Post-Tribune* reported the following day that a Missouri Pacific switch engine "was leaving (Russellville) for Eldon [when] the engine struck a weak spot in the track, a rail gave way and the engine rolled over an embankment."

On March 24, 1937, the *Central Missourian* reported, "The Engineer, O.P. King, was injured about the head and sustained body bruises. He was taken to the office of Dr. Leslie here for emergency treatment. His injuries were not serious." The fireman was not injured in the accident, and a wrecker was sent from Jefferson City to retrieve the damaged engine for repairs.

Although passenger service on the Bagnell Branch was suspended in the early 1930s, the line continued to be used for hauling freight. According to local historian L.A.B. Leslie, service was discontinued on the branch on August 15, 1962, and the tracks were later removed. The depot building remained in Russellville for many years but was demolished in the early 1970s to make room for what has since become Community Point Bank.

In the solitude of reflection on a bygone era, the *Miller County Autogram-Sentinel*, on January 12, 1954, penned these few simple and solemn words in tribute to a railroad possessing few surviving links to its rich legacy: "But the whistles are gone along with the railroad and only memories of yesteryears remain along the once booming Bagnell Branch."

NICHOLAS LINHARDT

Successful Stock Dealer and Farmer, Murdered in 1896

The commotion brought to the community of Lohman by the Missouri Pacific Railroad was overwhelmingly welcomed by local residents, who enjoyed seeing money flow through the hands of businessmen and neighbors. But this economic boost also resulted in a few warts in the community's history, including the grievous murder of one local resident for some cash he had earned selling livestock.

Nicholas "Nick" Linhardt was born in the Kingdom of Bavaria on September 19, 1841. When he was an infant, his parents fled the political turmoil in the future German state by immigrating to the United States and later settled in what became the predominantly German Lutheran community of Lohman.

"Christian [Nick's father] died when he was only a small boy," wrote Natalie Fischer Young in her family history book, *The Linhardts-Schuberts of Cole County: 1840–1980*. "He was raised by his step-father, Adam Schubert."

Service records reveal that during the Civil War, Nick Linhardt briefly served as a private in the Union forces of Company E, Forty-Second Regiment of the Enrolled Missouri Militia, under the command of Captain Charles Thompson. The part-time force had been raised to assist in the defense of the home regions of individuals like Linhardt, who had been compelled to serve in the regiments. After the war, Linhardt married Eva Marie Hager, a fellow Bavarian native. She helped raise the couple's growing family while her husband operated a sawmill and took care of their 420-acre farm a short distance outside of Lohman. Eventually, he became not only a successful farmer but also a wealthy stock dealer.

"It was the warm spring evening of April 30, 1896, when two Lohman area residents, John Blochberger and J.A.N. Linhardt, were returning home north of Lohman," said local historian Don Buchta. "Suddenly, the horses the two men rode became startled by something in the road. After settling down their horses, the two men dismounted to check out the object in their path."

Nicholas Linhardt is pictured with his wife, the former Eva Marie Hager. In 1896, Linhardt was murdered near Lohman for cash he earned through the sale of livestock. The culprit was captured and hanged in Jefferson City. *Natalie Fischer Young.*

What they discovered was the body of J.A.N. Linhardt's uncle, Nick Linhardt. He was barely breathing. The two observed wounds to Nick's skull and noticed blood pooled around the body and scattered upon the nearby grass.

"The two men also found a blood-stained wooden club about four feet long, lying near the road that had been traveled by Linhardt," Buchta said. "The badly beaten body, bloody club and empty wallet were all the evidence the two men needed to determine that a terrible crime had been committed."

Nick Linhardt was immediately taken to Lohman but died a short time later without ever regaining consciousness. Sheriff Samuel H. Sone in Jefferson City received a telegraph telling him to come to Lohman and begin the search for the murderer. Soon, Ed McKenzie, a man who had been employed by Linhardt for several years but had left his employment about a month prior to the murder, was observed freely spending cash in Jefferson City. He purchased sixty cents of meat at a meat shop and told the proprietor to keep the rest for when his wife needed to purchase more. McKenzie was also seen with a large roll of bills when purchasing clothing at a local store and, when questioned by the owner as to where he acquired it, remarked that he had been successful in a game of poker the previous night.

"These facts became known to Policeman Frank Henderson, who at once concluded that McKenzie was the man wanted for the robbery and murder at Lohman," wrote Natalie Fischer Young in her family history book.

The evidence continued to stack up against McKenzie, and he was soon placed under arrest at his home behind a saloon in Jefferson City. At the time of his apprehension, he was found feasting upon boxes of strawberries and surrounded by several valuable purchases but with only eighty-five cents in his possession. Further investigation revealed that McKenzie had served a term in jail for attempting to shoot his uncle a few years earlier. Additionally, a woman who lived in the same house as the suspected murderer claimed that he did not return until four o'clock the morning of the crime.

Newspaper accounts from the period explained that McKenzie knew his former boss frequently had large sums of money in his possession after selling livestock at the markets.

"Shortly after McKenzie was incarcerated, he told Chief Henderson during interrogation that one Harvey Williams had committed the murder," wrote Don Buchta. "McKenzie said he was only an accomplice and had nothing to do with the murder."

Williams was exonerated with evidence and alibis, while McKenzie eventually confessed to having unilaterally committed the murder. With scores of incensed Lohman residents wishing to implement vigilante justice, Sheriff Sone had to place McKenzie in protective custody inside a cell at the Missouri State Penitentiary.

On May 3, 1896, Nick Linhardt was laid to rest in the cemetery of St. Paul's Lutheran Church in Lohman.

McKenzie was able to escape custody and, though briefly eluding authorities, was captured in New Orleans and returned to Jefferson City. Found guilty of first-degree murder, he was hanged alongside two other condemned men behind the jail, the site that is now the Jefferson City Police Department. In the years that followed, Nick's wife, Eva, never remarried and raised her six children north of Lohman. She passed away in 1913 and lies at rest alongside her husband.

Lohman remains a quiet hamlet tucked between the rolling hills of rural Cole County and, for many years, was humming with a thriving business scene. Yet it retains a dark undercurrent in its broad history—a disconcerting circumstance fueled by greed that resulted in the murder of a respected resident. Linhardt's gruesome death once shocked the community of Lohman and continues to serve as a tempestuous tale of crime that resonates through retellings by local residents.

RAILROAD PARK

Missouri Pacific Caboose Helps Share Story of Russellville's Railroad Legacy

Railroad Park in downtown Russellville serves as a open-air museum of sorts, preserving the community's rich legacy as a stop along the former Bagnell Branch of the Missouri Pacific Railroad. The focal point of this recreational area is a caboose resting upon property where the railroad ran several decades ago, representing hours of hard work and labor by many local residents who desired a tangible symbol of bygone railroad history.

"The Sesquicentennial Celebration held June 10, 11, & 12, 1988, was a great success and, in September, the committee met to discuss the profits from the celebration," wrote the late Don and Berniece Jungmeyer. "There was much discussion as to what could be purchased to commemorate the celebration. Several suggestions were made, one being a caboose."

Jack Casten, an employee of Union Pacific Railroad, secured a Missouri Pacific caboose for the community of Russellville. It was loaded on a trailer in Centertown on December 20, 1988, and moved to Russellville for display in City Park. *Jim and Eve Campbell.*

Jack Casten, a local resident who served two terms as Russellville's mayor, was a conductor for Union Pacific Railroad. He inquired through official company channels about the steps to be taken to acquire a caboose for his community.

"Not long after he made the inquiry, my husband was informed that the railroad had a surplus caboose," said Reta Casten. "A few weeks later, the committee learned the caboose was on its way to the old railroad stop in Centertown and that it could be picked up there."

On Saturday, October 15, 1988, a crew of eager local volunteers led by Casten traveled to Sandy Hook to pick up railroad ties and rails to be used to prepare the site where the caboose would soon be displayed. The use of a boom truck and trailer was donated to transport, load and unload the material. Three days later, with a caboose ready for pickup in Centertown, the sesquicentennial committee met again to determine the most suitable location for placement of the railroad car. Although several sites were discussed, the final decision was for it to be placed on school property, adjacent to a ball field and a tennis/basketball court. Preparations continued as volunteers toiled to ensure the site was ready by digging holes, pouring the pads and setting the rails. Jack Casten and Don Jungmeyer traveled to Centertown to remove items aboard the caboose to prepare it for transport along the highway.

"Anyone traveling from Centertown to Russellville saw a strange sight (on December 17, 1988) as two men with a 2x4 [two-inch-by-four-foot board] were going down the road, stopping here and there to measure," wrote Don and Berniece Jungmeyer. "Yes, Don and Jack were measuring to see how many wires would have to be raised for the caboose to pass under."

Reta Casten recalled, "The caboose was loaded on the back of a tractor trailer and brought down State Highway U to Russellville [on December 20, 1988]. The utility companies came out to elevate the electric lines along the way so that it could pass through without damaging the lines."

When the caboose arrived in Russellville following its forty-five-minute trip along the rural two-lane highway, it was placed on the prepared site and then welded to the tracks. The following spring, volunteers attached steps to the caboose.

For the next quarter century, the caboose became a point of interest for the community and essentially a playground for local kids, who enjoyed exploring its sparse interior. But since it was not located in an area consistently under the eye of watchful adults, windows were damaged, walls were spray painted and it fell into a state of disrepair. The caboose was located a short distance south of the original Bagnell Branch, having little connection to

In 1988, a crew of volunteers uses a crane to unload the caboose and set it on rails for display near Russellville City Park, where it remained for twenty-five years. *Jim and Eve Campbell.*

the town's railroad history. In 2013, during preparations for celebration of a major milestone in Russellville's history, a new group of volunteers came together to give the caboose a facelift and relocate to a site where it would have historical context.

"Early Wednesday morning the combined efforts of crews from Twehous Excavation, Scott's Crane Service and Larry Payne Excavation moved the caboose from Russellville City Park to its new home in the newly completed Railroad Park in its downtown," reported the *Russellville Rebel* newsletter on May 9, 2013. "The park is being created with donations, volunteers and grants. The hope is to have the first phase of the park complete by the June Engine Show and Frog Leg Festival to celebrate Russellville's 175th anniversary."

Situated a short distance east of the former railroad depot and near the original railroad tracks, the caboose has since been sandblasted and repainted. Railroad Park now has not only the caboose but also military memorials in addition to picnic tables, benches and a restored railroad icehouse.

Reflecting on her late husband's twenty-nine years of service with Union Pacific Railroad and involvement with helping coordinate the acquisition of the caboose, Reta Casten maintains it was a bittersweet moment seeing the railcar moved to Railroad Park several years ago.

"Jack adored trains and was so proud of all the volunteers that helped bring the caboose to town in 1988," she said. "When they moved it to Railroad Park in 2013, I initially had my reservations, but I realized it would bring more people to the downtown and help preserve the railroad legacy." She added, "Seeing the caboose now connects me to memories of him and his love of the railroad, and I know if he were here, he would have supported it because it helps improve the town."

Casten's Dairi Freeze

House Served as Drive-In Food/Ice Cream Business in Russellville in Late 1960s

As a young girl growing up on a farm near Olean, Reta Bond aimed to convince herself that she would move to St. Louis after graduating high school and never again "milk another cow or hoe potatoes." To an extent, she made good on her promise, meeting Jack Casten on a blind date while living in St. Louis. However, after the couple married in 1957, she soon ended up back in the country, where they later toiled to run a small drive-in business.

"We eventually purchased a home in Eldon," Reta said. "Jack and I had discussed opening a drive-in and it just so happened that a family who owned a gas station near the junction of Highway 54 and 17 said they would build us a building to rent, if we would run it."

They accepted the offer, and the first iteration of Casten's Dairi Freeze was up and running in the early 1960s. Their family kept the home in Eldon but moved into a small trailer behind the drive-in so they could stay nearby while operating the business during the peak spring and summer months. In high school, Reta had worked part time at an Eldon drive-in and as a waitress at Randall's Restaurant. At the restaurant, she wore a white uniform with a black apron. At home, her family had no running water, so she washed her uniform by hand and hung it out the window to dry while driving to work.

"Years later, I always wore a white uniform while working at our own drive-in because I just thought it looked more professional, but by then we had running water," she chuckled. "Jack had a full-time job, so I ran the drive-in during the day, and he helped in the evenings and weekends. He came home one day and said he had bought an old house in Russellville; the building looked just awful and was falling in."

Reta recalled that her husband maintained that the house could be rebuilt and used as both their home and a new drive-in. Selling their house in Eldon, they moved to Russellville in 1965 and spent the next several months busy with remodeling. When the drive-in opened, the largest part of their business came from traffic along State Route C traveling to and from the Lake of the Ozarks. Casten's Dairi Freeze quickly became a popular destination for tenderloins, footlong hot dogs, chili, ice cream, milkshakes, fries and other tasty foods and treats.

"The drive-in was located right on the highway across from Trinity Lutheran Church, and most of our business came from out of town," she said. "We did have some locals who would stop and eat every day, though It had a walk-up window, patio seating, tables and barstools on the inside, along with a pinball machine and jukebox."

Similar to their previous drive-in business, Jack worked a full-time job during the day while Reta, who was raising a young son and two daughters, ran the drive-in. She had help from Betty Payne and Ruby Shikles, two older local women, who helped her cook, waitress and, occasionally, babysit. "They were a great help and did whatever needed to be done," she said. "It worked out great for everyone because I needed the assistance, and they enjoyed just getting out and seeing people."

From 1965 to 1970, Jack and Reta Casten operated Casten's Dairi Freeze in Russellville. The drive-in sold tenderloin sandwiches, footlong hot dogs, ice cream, malts and other foods and treats. The drive-in benefited from traffic heading to and from the Lake of the Ozarks. *Reta Casten.*

There were also a number of local high school students who worked their first job at the drive-in, where they received advice from Reta "to make the customer feel important and always look busy."

One evening, Reta recalled, she and her husband were working inside the drive-in and heard a car pull up outside, honking the horn. When they peered out the serving window, they were surprised by the odd sight that greeted them.

"Elmer Enloe, one of our regular customers, was sitting in his car along with about a dozen pigs of various sizes," she laughed. "They were on his lap, on the dash, in the back seat and the passenger seat." She added, "He had been at the sale barn and purchased the pigs. He was on his way to his farm in Enon to drop them off but stopped by the drive-in to get a tenderloin sandwich, fries and a soda."

In 1970, Jack was hired by the railroad, so the couple made the decision to close the drive-in after running the Russellville location for five years. Reta later worked at the local MFA Exchange and then became a postmaster relief clerk at Russellville, Olean, Lohman and Centertown. Jack passed away in 2001 and was laid to rest in Enloe Cemetery.

The drive-in has long since been stripped of its advertising, the walk-in window enclosed and the remainder of the interior converted into a conventional home, where Reta continues to reside. The younger generations have no memory of Casten's Dairi Freeze, while many older residents vaguely recall its existence along State Route C. But for Reta, it remains an important, if only brief, facet of the local business history of the community.

"We were busy and did well along the highway, but we certainly never got rich from it," she said. "We were running the drive-in back in hard times, but everyone was in the same boat back then." In conclusion, she remarked, "The one memory that stands out for me is that everyone was friendly and supportive of us…and that was appreciated. It really was a close neighborhood that I still call my home."

ALVIN WEBER

World War II Veteran Established Successful Produce Business in Russellville

Alvin Weber was born on a small farm south of Russellville in 1911, where he and his three brothers were instilled with a rural work ethic at a very early age. As the years passed and the Great Depression began to carve away the country's economic comforts, Alvin found the means to scratch out a living until his efforts were interrupted by the country's call to arms.

"My dad had a twin brother, Alfred, and they both attended the nearby one-room Enterprise School," said Mark Weber. "He graduated the eighth grade and later moved to Lohman to open a produce business."

The young man started to purchase cream, eggs, milk and other produce from local farmers, selling them at a marginal profit locally while also making shipments to packaging houses via the Bagnell Branch of the Missouri Pacific Railroad. In 1936, Weber married Neva Eberhart from the Russellville area. The couple moved to Sedalia in 1939, where Alvin was employed to drive a truck for Swift & Company, a business that purchased and sold produce on an expanded scale.

"My parents decided to come back to Russellville in 1941 and opened Weber Produce," said Mark Weber. "He ran the business until February 1943, when he received notice that he was being inducted into the military for World War II."

According to Mark Weber, his father had registered for the military draft in Pettis County a couple of years earlier while still living in Sedalia. The February 26, 1943 edition of the *Sedalia Weekly Democrat* noted that Alvin Weber was among seventy-five local men "called into the Armed Forces" and "[o]rdered by the board to report on March 5 [1943]."

Less than two years into his new business endeavors, he shuttered Weber Produce in preparation for his departure for military service. He was inducted into the U.S. Army at Fort Leavenworth, Kansas, on March 6, 1943, and assigned to the Army Air Forces. Initially, he was sent to Florida to complete his basic training at the Miami Beach Training Center. From there, he traveled to Aberdeen, Maryland, for six weeks of advanced training to learn the maintenance of small weapons.

"He did a lot of training stateside that included gunnery training in the Mojave Desert," said Mark Weber. "Later, he also trained at Ardmore, Oklahoma; Dalhart Army Air Base, Texas; and in Russell, Kansas."

The instruction and training helped prepare Weber for performance as an armorer for the Boeing B-29 Superfortress, a four-engine heavy bomber. His military records indicate that he supervised five personnel, all of whom were trained to work on the flight line inspecting the guns on the aircraft and making any necessary repairs to keep the weapons in a peak operational condition.

Assigned to the 458th Bomb Squadron of the 330th Bomb Group, Weber deployed to North Field on Guam in January 1945. For the next several

Alvin Weber served on Guam with the U.S. Army Air Forces in World War II. He became a respected businessman in Russellville, also serving on the town council and helping establish the local Lion's Club. *Mark Weber.*

months, Weber and his crew not only maintained the small guns on the aircraft but also loaded and prepared the bombs for their assorted strategic bombing missions against Japanese targets. Although his primary duty was on the flight line at Guam, Weber also performed duty on the islands of Saipan and Tinian. On one occasion, he had the opportunity to locate and visit with his younger brother Tony, who was serving with the army on Saipan.

Mark Weber said, "After the war came to an end, the 458th participated in a show of force during the Japanese surrender in Tokyo Bay on September 2, 1945. On that day, my father flew on a B-29 loaded with bombs because the U.S. did not entirely trust the Japanese. After the Japanese officially surrendered, my dad's bomber dropped its bombs in the ocean during the return flight."

The thirty-four-year-old staff sergeant returned to the United States on February 6, 1946, receiving his honorable discharge at Jefferson Barracks in St. Louis a week later. Reuniting with his wife in Russellville, he soon reopened Weber Produce and began the process of reintegrating into his community. In the years after the war, he and his wife raised two sons, John and Mark. In 1954, Weber erected a new building and expanded his offerings to include products such as feed, grains, seeds and veterinary supplies in addition to performing custom grinding and mixing.

Weber's spirit of public service included involvement in many worthwhile projects. In later years, he served on the local school board, helped establish the Lion's Club in Russellville and was a longtime member of the town council. Additionally, he helped form the Russellville Rural Fire Association and was a volunteer firefighter for many years.

"In 1973, the [Weber Produce] business was sold to Neal and Mary Crawford, who changed the name to Crawford Feed and Farm Supply," noted Russellville's sesquicentennial book.

A member of Trinity Lutheran Church in Russellville, Weber was ninety-four years old when he passed away in 2006. He and his wife are interred in Enloe Cemetery west of Russellville. When pondering his father's participation in World War II, Mark Weber noted that little was ever spoken about his experiences in the Western Pacific, but his father demonstrated a number of commendable traits that made him an individual worthy of admiration.

"Dad always struck me as someone who was solid as a rock," he said. "Although I am sure he had things that he worried about, if and when he did worry, he never revealed it around us." He added, "He was also a man of great faith, and I always looked up to him because I was proud of everything he represented and accomplished."

Dr. E.M. Eberhart

Provided Range of Medical Services to Russellville Area

Russellville and several outlying communities were blessed for more than four decades with the medical knowledge of Dr. Elbert Meredith Eberhart. His journey from Pennsylvania to the rural areas of mid-Missouri was an unexpected adventure influenced by war that later cemented his reputation as a caring physician and a "one-stop doc."

Born on January 14, 1914, and raised in Milton, Pennsylvania, Eberhart went on to graduate from Milton High School. He then chose to pursue a career in medicine by enrolling at Bucknell University, where he played baseball and basketball. While in college, he met Anne Johnson, a teacher living and working in Lewisburg, Virginia, and the couple married in 1936.

"My father then transferred to the Kirksville [Missouri] College of Osteopathy and Surgery to earn his medical degree," said Salle Eberhart, the late doctor's daughter.

According to the June 3, 1940 edition of the *Daily Item* (Sunbury, Pennsylvania), Eberhart was finishing up his initial medical education by interning at Laughlin Hospital in Kirksville when the approaching war unexpectedly shifted the direction of his career.

"During World War II, instead of his induction into the military, the government sent my father to Russellville, where he was to serve a couple of years as a doctor for the community," Salle Eberhart explained. "Another reason he was sent to Russellville was because there were some older doctors in the area who were retiring," she added.

Dr. Eberhart and his family arrived in Russellville in November 1940 and began to practice medicine while also raising a son and a daughter. He fell in love with the community and began operating his practice out of a small brick building with three rooms, heated by a potbelly stove.

Meredith Eberhart, grandson and namesake of the late doctor, said, "I would come up during the summers and go with him when he made house calls to the Mennonites by Versailles. Oftentimes, he would come back with freshly baked pies and hand-sewn quilts as payment for his services." He continued, "I can also remember that he had a couple of freezers in his basement full of beef—his house was like a grocery store because of the way he received payment for his medical services. My grandfather was also a one-stop doctor—he had an X-ray machine, pharmacy, physical therapy and delivered babies as well."

In 1964, Dr. Eberhart moved his practice into a larger clinic housed within a row of historic brick buildings in downtown Russellville. Although this added space provided him with a laboratory, treatment rooms and much-needed space, he continued to make house calls and respond to emergencies at all hours of the night.

"There was a time when he had an offer to join another doctor practicing in a clinic in St. Louis," said his daughter. "Although that would have meant a lot more income for him, it never was about the money. He simply fell in love with the town, its people and helping out whenever he could."

With polio outbreaks threatening many communities in the United States, the doctor was on the front lines and battled the spread of the deadly disease by hosting clinics in the Russellville area to administer vaccinations in the late 1950s. According to reflections of some area residents, Dr. Eberhart might lend a sympathetic ear to a high school student experiencing relationship issues, while other times providing an osteopathic manipulation for someone experiencing back pain. On one occasion, he was called upon to reattach the fingertip of a young man injured in an accident at the local farmer's exchange. However, Dr. Eberhart's engagement with the community extended beyond the medical field. He was elected to serve many terms on the school board in Russellville, dedicated to ensuring local students received the best education possible. In his spare time, the doctor also enjoyed chatting about basketball and spending time outdoors, either hunting quail or fishing.

In 1975, Dr. Eberhart and his first wife divorced. He later married Mildred Steenbergen, and the couple, in their later years, often attended church services at nearby Mt. Olive Baptist Church.

Dr. E.M. Eberhart became the physician for the Russellville area after graduating medical school 1940. He made house calls and provided a full range of medical care to the community. *Salle Eberhart.*

"It wasn't a situation where he would schedule one patient right after the other to see as many as possible within a day," said Salle Eberhart. "He cared deeply about his patients and spent a lot of time at their homes, visiting with them at their kitchen tables and trying to provide a little comfort, especially if someone in the family was dying."

Following her graduation from high school, Salle went on to attend nursing school and pursued that career path for a number of decades. It was a decision, she maintained, inspired by her own father's service as a physician in the local community.

Ever the outdoorsman, Dr. Eberhart died from a heart attack on October 24, 1984, while cutting wood. He was interred in Enloe Cemetery near the community of Russellville, where he had contentedly spent the largest part of his life among his patients, neighbors and friends.

"They just don't make doctors like my father anymore—he treated the entire body and mind," said Salle, when reflecting on her father's auspicious medical career. "And I said before, he wasn't here for the money; he loved the town and the people. He was truly dedicated to the medical profession and cared about his patients. In the days before insurance, he made sure everyone received the care they needed despite their ability to pay."

Freeman Kraus

Farmer, Truck Driver and Feed Store Owner
Leaves Area Youth with Fond Memories

Freeman Kraus was a respected farmer and business owner who possessed ties to small communities in both Cole and Moniteau Counties. Often, he is remembered for allowing local youth to accompany him on livestock deliveries to St. Louis and for owning a quaint feedstore in Enon, where local residents could purchase farm supplies and swap stories over a cold soda. As a second-generation American citizen, Kraus occasionally reflected upon his father's efforts to instill an appreciation for certain aspects of their German heritage.

"My father and his sister, Ona Marie, grew up on a farm outside of Russellville," recalled Kraus's only child, Martha Jobe. "When they came in from doing farm work, his father would read to them from the Bible in German every day at lunch."

In 1920, when Kraus turned six years old, he began attending school in Russellville. At the time, the local education system was undergoing transformations, since funding was limited and space for classes posed a recurring challenge for community leaders. In the years prior to his passing, Kraus wrote some of his reflections of his early educational experiences, explaining that although a two-story brick grade school building had been constructed, his first two years of schooling were in a building rented from the Catholic Church because of overcrowding. When beginning third grade in 1922, Kraus wrote, his class "moved to the grade school building, which was much better." He added, "There was a nice big level playground," and much excitement occurred when his class "got to go to [Jefferson City] to [visit] the Capitol."

Life passed quickly for the young student. He remembered his fifth through eighth grade classes being held in a room on the second floor of the large brick school building. It was during this time frame that a longtime local teacher, Archie Russell, demonstrated his intolerance for misbehavior among his students.

"Vernie Kellogg and Paul Emmerich had trouble on the school ground at recess one day when the teacher [Russell] was gone," wrote Kraus. "The boys decided to go to an alley, which was close to the school, and settle their troubles, in fact, fight it out."

Since the alley was opposite the direction that Kraus walked home, and he did not know what was going on, he missed witnessing the fight. His teacher, who lived in a home next to the school, later heard about the scuffle and came to school the next day with an armful of switches.

Kraus recalled, "When school took up, they raised the doors between the rooms and all the girls went into the other room and all the boys came to Archie's room. He made a little speech and he whipped everybody but Foster [Scrivner] and I."

L.A.B. Leslie wrote in Russellville's sesquicentennial book that the community was without a high school from 1929 to 1931. This necessitated that Kraus travel to the community of Olean to finish his high school education, graduating in 1933.

"I know for a while he worked construction on Highway 54," said Martha Jobe, evoking past discussions shared with her father. "Apparently, he was paid a little more because he used his own team of mules. Later, he worked several years at the MFA Exchange in Russellville and drove a truck for them."

Kraus was soon able to purchase his own truck and operated a business making livestock deliveries to St. Louis for local farmers. When the MFA Exchange in Enon came up for sale, he purchased it and opened his own feed store.

"My mother, Thelma Dawson, married my father on June 8, 1941," said

Jobe. "She was a schoolteacher for many years, and for a while, they lived in a house next to the old Enon Bank. Later, they moved to his father-in-law's farm outside of Enon and built a new house, where they remained for the rest of their years."

Jobe noted that her father farmed with his father-in-law for many years, in addition to making livestock deliveries to St. Louis and operating Kraus Feed and Fertilizer.

"When I turned fifteen or sixteen years old, my dad thought that my summer job should be to work in the store," Jobe said. "He would leave to tend to other business and locals would come in and tell me what they needed. Then I would write up the bill, collect their payment and they would load it." She added, "The store also became quite the local gathering place,

Freeman Kraus was well known in the Enon area for the feed store he operated and for allowing local youth to accompany him on livestock deliveries to St. Louis. *Martha Jobe.*

and people would come to visit and catch up on what was going on around the area."

Jobe's father served many years on the board of the former Community Bank of Russellville (now Community Point Bank) in addition to the board for Enloe Cemetery. A man of faith, Kraus volunteered as a deacon with Mt. Olive Baptist Church. In 2002, the eighty-eight-year-old farmer and businessman passed away and is interred in Enloe Cemetery. In the years following her father's death, Jobe penned several recollections about the positive influence her father had on so many young people in the Enon community.

"Dad was farmer first—all of his other business interests were secondary to that," Jobe recalled. "When my father died, I was truly amazed at the number of friends who came to pay their respects and tell me they would always remember a time in their youth when (dad) had taken them on their first trip to St. Louis (on a livestock delivery). For many of them, it had been their first trip without parents, first time to ride in a 'big truck,' or the first time to eat in a restaurant. The experiences and conversations had made it an event they [would] always remember."

Thelma Kraus

Dedicated Teacher Enjoyed a Thirty-Five-Year Career in Mid-Missouri Schools

On the frigid evening of January 24, 1915, a baby girl was born on a small farm south of Russellville. Three years later, Thelma Dawson moved with her parents to a farm near the small Moniteau County community of Enon. While living in the area, she met the man who became her husband and embarked upon a multidecade career as an educator, spanning one-room schoolhouses, the Russellville school system and Jefferson City Public Schools. Coming of age in the years prior to the Great Depression, Thelma Kraus penned some reflections about a few of her experiences as an only child on a small Missouri farm.

"Chores consisted of feeding the chickens, gathering the eggs, feeding the pigs and milking a cow," she recalled. "Of course, the mules were unharnessed and put out to pasture or put in the barn if they were needed the next day."

Her education was received at the former New Zion School, a one-room school located a mile east of Enon. At an early age, she decided to become a teacher and, after graduating from Olean High School in 1934 as the valedictorian of her class, she was hired to teach at nearby Valley Home School in rural Cole County. In notes written before her passing, Kraus recalled, "We took the teacher's examinations that covered every area that we would be required to teach. In August [1934] I started my career of school teaching—I had students from first grade through eighth grade in one room. I had no experience except Sunday School classes I taught at church."

Receiving a forty-dollar monthly salary, Kraus began attending summer classes at Central Missouri State College in Warrensburg, remaining in college for two years and earning her teaching certificate and sixty hours of college credit.

"[In 1935] I applied for the teaching position at Lincoln School in Moniteau County and was hired for $55 a month—$15 more than my first job," Kraus recalled. "I stayed at Lincoln four years, then taught in Olean one year, grades one through four."

Kraus was hired to teach at Russellville for the 1940–41 school year.

Thelma Kraus graduated as valedictorian of her class at Olean High School in 1934. She taught for thirty-five years at several schools, eventually retiring from Jefferson City Public Schools. *Martha Jobe.*

However, since a new school building was being constructed, she spent her first year in a one-room schoolhouse located behind Trinity Lutheran Church. While still in college, she began dating Freeman Kraus, an Enon resident and fellow graduate of Olean, whom she married on June 8, 1941.

She wrote, "Because I was a married woman, my husband was supposed to be able to support a wife. The rural schools did not have that ruling so, in August 1942, I started teaching in New Zion school, where I had attended."

In 1945, new rulings required a college degree to teach. Kraus had not attended college since 1937 but had earned sixty hours of college credit and her teaching certificate. Believing her teaching career to be over, she was asked to teach at Russellville High School in 1946 and issued a one-year teaching certificate by the Department of Education. Spending one year teaching freshman and sophomore classes, she left her education career in 1947 after her temporary certificate expired. She would later be granted additional temporary certificates and spend a total of fifteen years as a teacher at Russellville.

Martha Jobe, the only child of the Krauses, noted, "My parents eventually moved to the farm that was owned by my mother's parents, and that's where they lived the rest of their lives. My mother continued teaching while my dad farmed and also ran a feedstore and livestock delivery business. My mother was my third grade teacher at Russellville, and during that school year, she had as many as forty-seven students in her class. During that time, she earned her degree in education [in 1958] attending night and summer classes at Lincoln University, as well as keeping up with the usual farm chores."

The final stretch of Kraus's career came in 1967, when she was hired by the Jefferson City Public School System. She retired in 1977 while teaching at West Elementary School. Throughout the years, she remained an active member of the Jefferson City Community Teachers Association and the Missouri State Teachers Association. Her dedication to teaching extended to the weekends as a member of Mt. Olive Baptist Church near Russellville, where she instructed Sunday School classes and sang with the choir.

"Mr. and Mrs. David Jobe…honored her parents, Freeman and Thelma (Dawson) Kraus who celebrated their 50th wedding anniversary June 9, with a reception at Mt. Olive Baptist Church in Russellville," reported the *Eldon Advertiser* on June 20, 1991. "Approximately 300 relatives and friends attended the reception."

Thelma Kraus was eighty-one years old when she passed away on April 7, 1996, and is interred in Enloe Cemetery near Russellville; her husband died six years later. Her many years of teaching and community involvement left unique impressions upon local youth, many of which remain effortlessly evoked.

"Thelma was my neighbor, Sunday school teacher and third grade teacher at Russellville," recalled Marvin Proctor. "After I received my teaching degree, she had transferred to the Jefferson City School System, and we carpooled together to work since I was teaching in JC also." He added, "She would read license plates and tell whose car it was by the plate number, not by make or color. It was also widely known by those in the community that she was able to remember individual birthdates by the dozens, if not hundreds—she was a numbers genius. My time with the Krauses has left many cherished memories and I was fortunate to have these people in my life."

Bibliography

Central Missourian. "M.A. Switch Engine Rolls into Ditch." March 24, 1937.

Daily Capital News. "Russellville." November 17, 1920.

———. "Russellville Grad Addresses '47 Class." May 30, 1947.

———. "St. Paul's Celebrates 125th Year." July 30, 1977.

Daily Item. "E.M. Eberhart, Milton, Graduates from School." June 3, 1940.

"Dr. W.C. Hatler." *Medical Review: A Weekly Retrospect of Medicine and Surgery* 25, no. 10 (March 5, 1892): 197.

Eldon Advertiser. "Local Happenings." November 18, 1915.

———. "Three Hundred Attend 50th Anniversary." June 20, 1991.

Grabert, Donald L. *History of the Third Infantry Division.* Paducah, KY: Turner Publishing Company, 1988.

Iberia Sentinel. "Work Starts on Russellville's New $96,000 School Building." December 14, 1939.

Illustrated Sketchbook & Directory of Jefferson City and Cole County, Missouri, 1900. Capital City Family Research, 1900.

Jefferson City Post-Tribune. "Widely Known Cole Man Dies." September 14, 1938.

Koester, Reba A. *The Heritage of Russellville in Cole County.* Jefferson City, MO: self-published, 1977.

Lawrence Chieftain. "Dr. Hatler." May 19, 1892.

McDowell, Erin. "The Rise and Fall of Movie Theaters." *Business Insider.* May 26. 2020. https://www.businessinsider.com/photos-that-show-the-rise-and-fall-of-movie-theaters-2020-5.

Miller County Autogram-Sentinel. "Cumberland Presbyterian." August 6, 1885.

———. "Local Happenings." May 30, 1895.

———. "O.C. Wright Tells of Early Bagnell Line." January 12, 1954.

———. "Tellmans Interested in Kansas Oil." December 9, 1920.

Mydland, Leidulf. "The Legacy of One-Room Schoolhouses: A Comparative Study of the American Midwest and Norway." *European Journal of American Studies* 6, no. 1 (Spring 2011).

Partridge, Eric. *A Dictionary of Catch Phrases*. Lanham, MD: Scarborough House, 1992.

People's Tribune. "Local Affairs." July 2, 1873.

Raithel, Erna. *Russellville, Missouri, Sesquicentennial: 1838–1988*. Versailles, MO: B-W Graphics, Inc. 1988.

Ruskin, John. *The Seven Lamps of Architecture*. London: Smith, Elder, 1849.

Ruston Daily Leader. "Cherry Pie Champ." April 10, 1936.

Scheperle, Palmer. *History of the Scheperle (Schepperle) Family of America*. Jefferson City, MO: Modern-Litho Print, 1982.

Sedalia Weekly Bazoo. "Twenty Years After: A Prominent Missourian Arrested for the Murder of an Indian." September 4, 1890.

Sedalia Weekly Democrat. "Seventy-Five Called to Armed Forces." February 26, 1943.

———. "Three Died in an Accident on Way Home from Fair." August 23, 1929.

Society of the Third Infantry Division. "History of the Third Infantry Division." Accessed January 2, 2022. https://www.society3rdid.org/3rd-division-history.

St. John's Lutheran Church. *Founded on the Rock, Forward in Faith, 150 Years: 1867–2017*. Jefferson City, MO: Brown Printing, 2017.

St. Louis Globe-Democrat. "A Ride to Death." December 19, 1881.

St. Louis Post-Dispatch. "Want the Boys Punished." October 4, 1897.

———. "Wants a Pardon: Dr. W.C. Hatler Undergoing an Unrighteous Sentence." February 21, 1892.

St. Paul's Lutheran Church. *125th Anniversary: 1852–1977*. Lohman, MO: self-published, 1977.

Sunday News and Tribune. "A.N. Linhardt to Sell Farm Supplies Here." December 8, 1935.

———. "Ghost Town 'Alive,' at Least in Memory." July 18, 1971.

———. "Russellville Sets Benefit Tilt January 16." January 10, 1965.

Trinity Evangelical Lutheran Church. *Golden Jubilee: 1895–1945*. Russellville, MO: self-published, November 1945.

———. *Sixtieth Anniversary: 1895–1955*. Russellville, MO: self-published, November 13, 1955.

Warman-Stallings, Kelly. *The Ghost Towns of Central Missouri, Volume 1*. Jefferson City, MO: Ketch's Printing, 1993.

Young, Natalie A. *The Linhardts-Schuberts of Cole County, Missouri: 1840–1980*. St. Louis, MO: self-published, 1980.

INDEX

About the Author

Jeremy P. Ämick has for years chronicled in writing the legacy of United States military veterans, past and present. He has authored the books *Camp Crowder*, *Missouri in World War I* and *Missouri Veterans: Monuments and Memorials*. A veteran of the U.S. Army and Missouri National Guard, he is the recipient of the Jefferson Award for public service and makes his home in Russellville, Missouri, along with his wife, Tina.

Visit us at
www.historypress.com